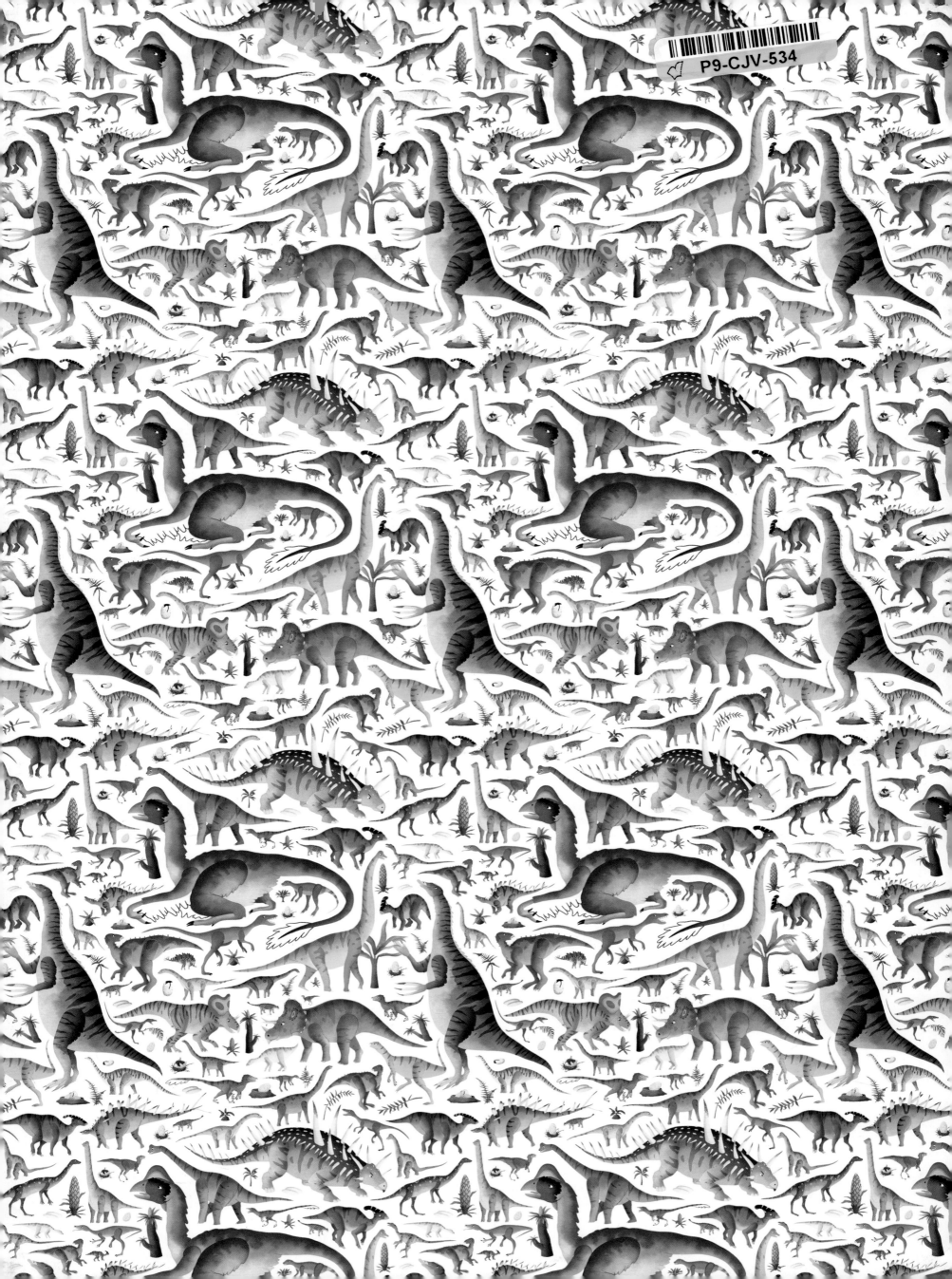

# ATLAS OF DINOSAUR ADVENTURES

WIDE EYED EDITIONS

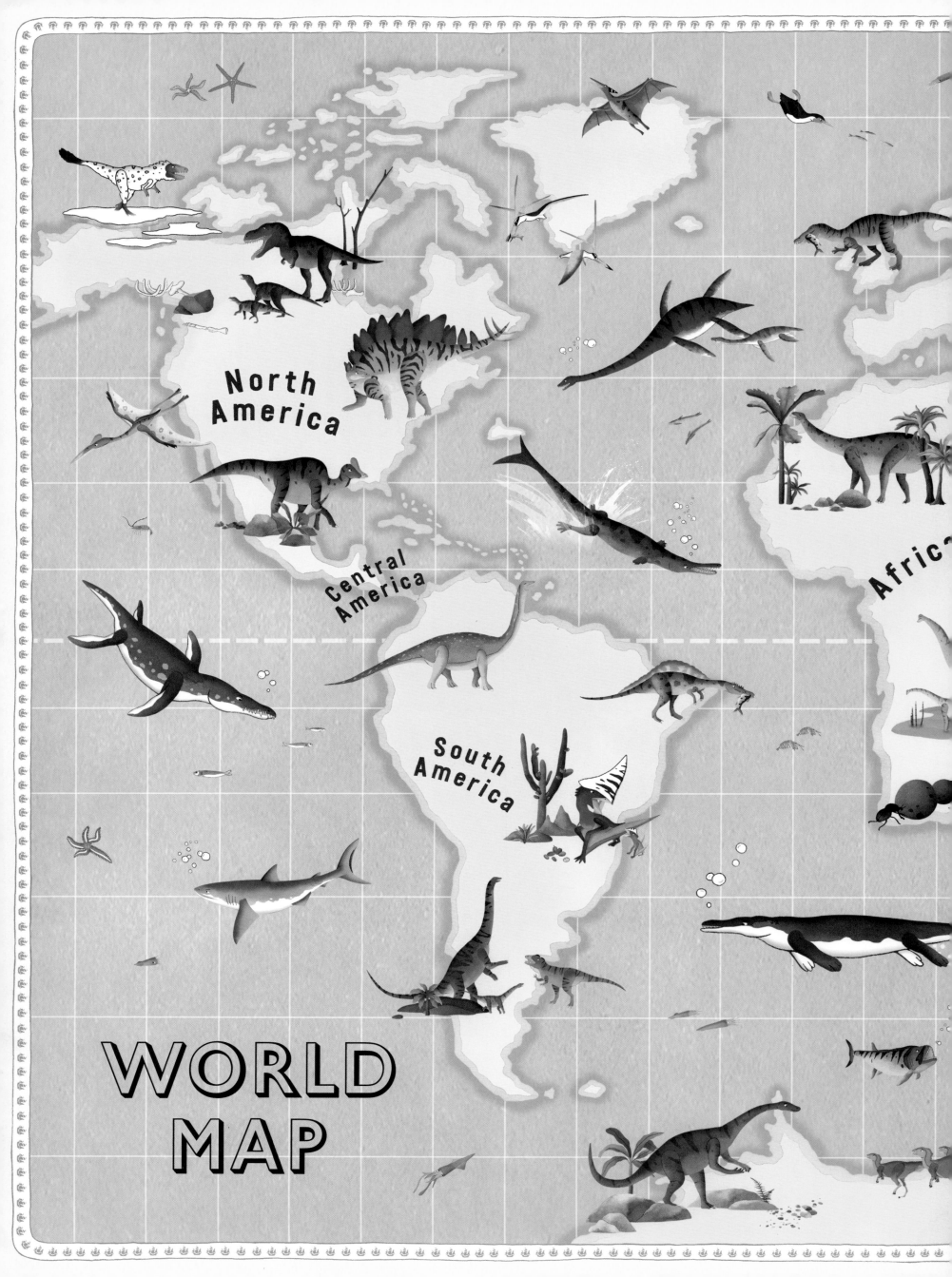

North
America

Central
America

Africa

South
America

WORLD
MAP

Europe

Asia

Middle
East

Australasia
& Oceania

Antarctica

N
W        E
S

# CONTENTS

# EMBARK ON A PREHISTO

**Apatosaurus**

**Stegosaurus**

**Deinonychus**

**Nothronychus**

**Triceratops**

**T. rex**

**Pteranodon**

**Archelon**

**Pterodaustro**

**Argentinosaurus**

**Giganotosaurus**

**Caiuajara**

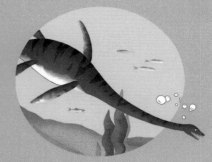

**Plesiosaurus**

**Baryonyx**

**Mosasaurus**

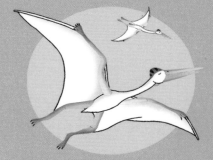

**Hatzegopteryx**

**Coelophysis**

**Giraffatitan**

**Kentrosaurus**

**Sarcosuchus**

# RIC ADVENTURE...

**Spinosaurus**

**Microraptor**

**Gigantoraptor**

**Oviraptor**

**Leaellynasaura**

Hundreds of millions of years ago, long before humans existed, a group of extraordinary creatures dominated the planet: the dinosaurs. They included some of the most enormous animals ever to walk the Earth, as well as some of the most fearsome hunters.

Alongside the dinosaurs lived other incredible animals, such as the pterosaurs who ruled the skies, and the deadly marine reptiles who prowled the seas.

This book will take you on an adventure back in time to the days of the dinosaurs. With every turn of the page, you'll meet a different creature and discover its amazing behaviours, from cunning hunting techniques to clever defence tactics and epic migrations. Come and explore – a world of prehistoric wonders awaits!

**Muttaburrasaurus**

**Sinornithoides**

**Psittacosaurus**

**Ginsu shark**

**Charonosaurus**

**Antarctopelta**

# WORLD OF THE DINOSAURS

The dinosaurs lived during a time called the Mesozoic era, which is divided up into three stages: the Triassic, Jurassic and Cretaceous periods. Back then, the world looked very different from how it looks today. The Earth's crust is made up of giant pieces, called tectonic plates. Beneath the crust is a layer of hot rock, which slowly swirls around, gradually moving the continents on top. About 250 million years ago, the continents were joined together as one huge piece of land: a supercontinent called Pangaea.

### THE TRIASSIC WORLD
**(252–201 MILLION YEARS AGO)**

The first dinosaurs appeared in the Triassic period. For most of this time, the continents were joined together in the supercontinent of Pangaea. The climate was hot and dry, with large areas of desert. Towards the end of the Triassic period, Pangaea started to break up.

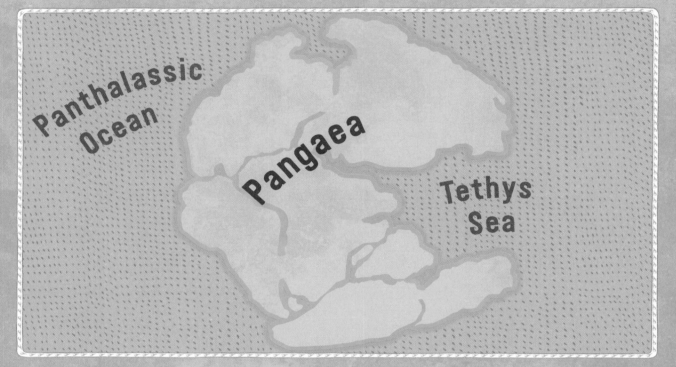

### THE JURASSIC WORLD
**(201–145 MILLION YEARS AGO)**

In the Jurassic period, Pangaea split in two to make the continents of Laurasia and Gondwana. Rainfall turned the deserts into lush forests, and shallow seas flooded some of the land. The giants of the dinosaur world — the sauropods — appeared in the Jurassic period.

# Fossil Finds

How do we know about the dinosaurs? Because we have found their fossils — their preserved remains — buried underground. By studying these remains, scientists can find out a lot about creatures from millions of years ago. The best fossils come from places where dinosaurs were quickly buried by wet mud after they died.

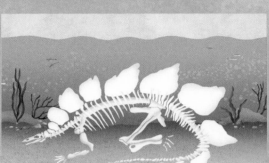

1) A dinosaur dies and its body is washed or falls into a lake or river and sinks to the bottom. The animal's flesh rots away, leaving only the skeleton behind.

2) Mud and sand cover the skeleton. Over millions of years, layers build up and turn into rock. Minerals seep into the dinosaur's bones, turning them to stone.

3) Movements of the Earth's crust lift the fossil up to the surface. The top layers of rock are worn away by wind and rain, exposing the fossil, ready to be found.

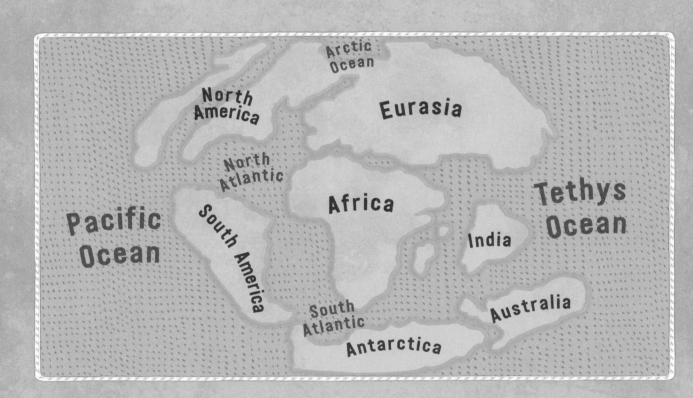

## THE CRETACEOUS WORLD
### (145–66 MILLION YEARS AGO)

The continents continued to drift apart and became separated by large oceans: the world began to look like the one we know today. Many dinosaur species flourished, including Tyrannosaurus rex and Triceratops. But by the end of the Cretaceous period, all the dinosaurs had died out.

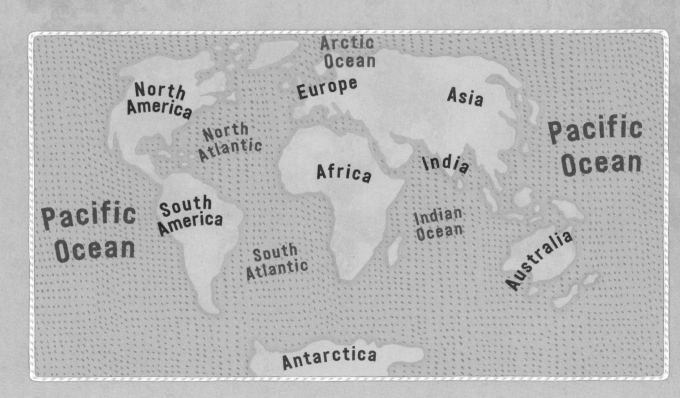

## THE WORLD TODAY

The continents that we know today have moved so much since the early days of the dinosaurs. And they are still on the move! The earth beneath our feet is moving slowly at a speed of up to 12 centimetres per year. In another hundred million years the planet will look different again.

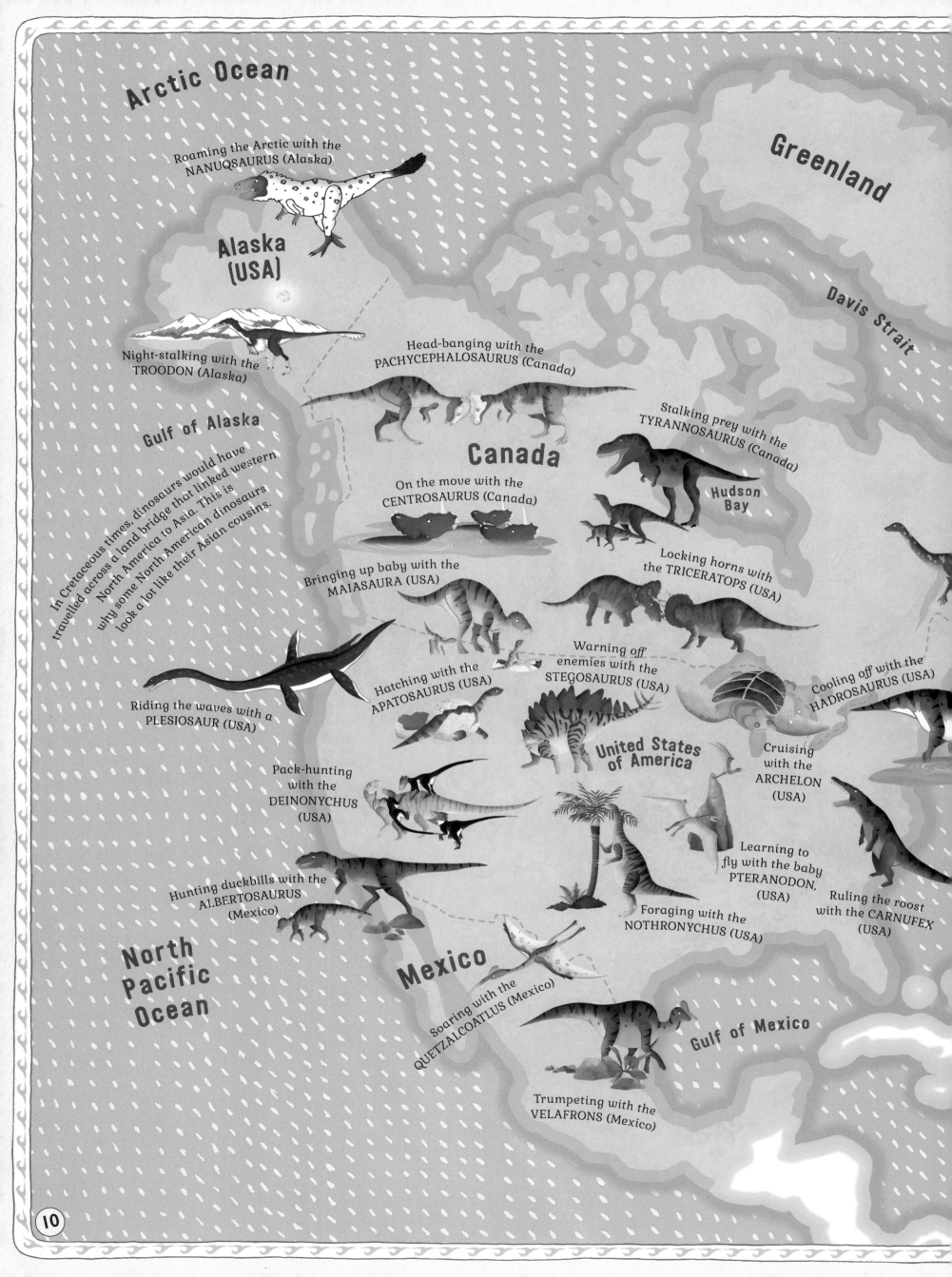

Arctic Ocean

Greenland

Roaming the Arctic with the
NANUQSAURUS (Alaska)

Alaska
(USA)

Davis Strait

Night-stalking with the
TROODON (Alaska)

Head-banging with the
PACHYCEPHALOSAURUS (Canada)

Stalking prey with the
TYRANNOSAURUS (Canada)

Gulf of Alaska

Canada

Hudson
Bay

On the move with the
CENTROSAURUS (Canada)

In Cretaceous times, dinosaurs would have travelled across a land bridge that linked western North America to Asia. This is why some North American dinosaurs look a lot like their Asian cousins.

Locking horns with
the TRICERATOPS (USA)

Bringing up baby with the
MAIASAURA (USA)

Cooling off with the
HADROSAURUS (USA)

Warning off
enemies with the
STEGOSAURUS (USA)

Hatching with the
APATOSAURUS (USA)

Riding the waves with a
PLESIOSAUR (USA)

United States
of America

Cruising
with the
ARCHELON
(USA)

Pack-hunting
with the
DEINONYCHUS
(USA)

Learning to
fly with the baby
PTERANODON,
(USA)

Hunting duckbills with the
ALBERTOSAURUS (Mexico)

Foraging with the
NOTHRONYCHUS (USA)

Ruling the roost
with the CARNUFEX
(USA)

North
Pacific
Ocean

Mexico

Soaring with the
QUETZALCOATLUS (Mexico)

Gulf of Mexico

Trumpeting with the
VELAFRONS (Mexico)

10

# NORTH AMERICA

**Rich in fossils, North America is a dinosaur-hunter's dream, especially in the 'badland' states on the west coast of the USA, where the rocks have yielded spectacular prehistoric finds. This continent was home to a rich array of prehistoric creatures, including some of the most iconic dinosaurs: from the terrifying T. rex to the spiky Stegosaurus.**

The states of Utah, Wyoming, Montana and Colorado are hot spots for fossil-hunters. This is because they have large, dry areas of rock where the surface has been worn away, revealing hidden dino treasures.

Plodding with the
ANCHISAURUS
(Canada)

Bermuda

North
Atlantic
Ocean

Sargasso
Sea

Caribbean Sea

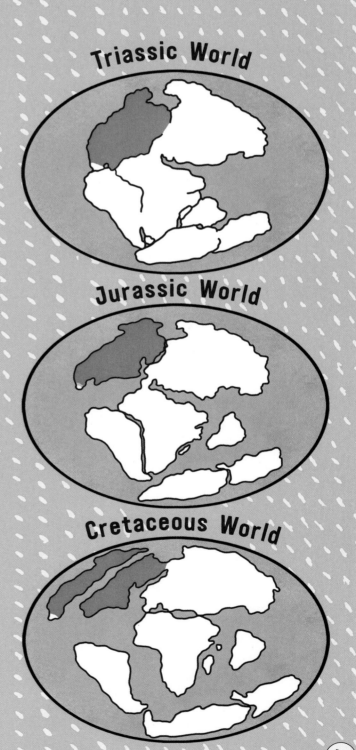

Triassic World

Jurassic World

Cretaceous World

In the Cretaceous period, western and eastern North America were divided by a shallow ocean, filled with ancient sea creatures.

USA

Dinosaur National Monument

In 1879, a fossil-hunter discovered a dino that he named Brontosaurus. In 1903, it was decided that Brontosaurus was the same as another dinosaur called Apatosaurus. Recently, though, a new study has suggested that the two might be different after all!

This fierce meat-eater, called Ceratosaurus, had such long teeth that you could see them poking out even when its mouth was shut!

A female Apatosaurus may have laid small clutches of eggs in different nesting sites. If one site was discovered by hungry egg-eaters, hopefully the other eggs would survive elsewhere.

A baby Apatosaurus weighed less than 5 kilograms, but by the time it was 30, it would have been about 10,000 times heavier!

These youngsters had to grow quickly because the bigger they were, the better chance they had of escaping from hunters.

## HATCHING WITH THE
# APATOSAURUS, USA

About 152 million years ago on the outskirts of a deep forest, there's a stirring in the undergrowth. From the fern-covered forest floor, a little snout pokes slowly up, followed by a long neck. A tiny Apatosaurus hatchling emerges, blinking, into the light. About ten weeks ago, the mother laid a small clutch of football-sized eggs here, buried out of sight. Now this youngster has hatched, it must be on its guard, for danger is everywhere.

As its siblings hatch around it, the baby notices a deadly Ceratosaurus pacing through the trees. Luckily, the small size and camouflage colours of the Apatosaurus mean that it escapes the hunter's notice. But the little ones must quickly retreat into the forest if they are to stay safe. There they will begin eating huge amounts of foliage every day so they can grow into some of the most enormous creatures ever to walk the Earth!

The Apatosaurus belonged to a family of huge plant-eaters called sauropods. Its massive body was supported by thick, tree-trunk-like legs.

A full-grown Apatosaurus was longer than two London buses parked end to end.

The mother Apatosaurus laid her eggs on the edge of the forest because her huge body meant that she couldn't travel deeper into the woods.

The teeth of an Apatosaurus were like the prongs on a rake. This huge creature used them to scrape leaves from the branches.

At times of its fastest growth, a young Apatosaurus put on up to 14 kilograms per day — the same weight as an average 3-year-old child!

### Apatosaurus

**Meaning:** 'Deceptive lizard' (because its bones looked like those of a sea creature called a mosasaur)
**First Fossil Found:** USA
**Date:** Late Jurassic
**Group:** Sauropods
**Diet:** Plants
**Size:** 23 metres long

USA

Dinosaur Ridge

This tiny pterosaur, Anurognathus, was a cousin of the dinosaurs. It would have hunted insects including lacewings and dragonflies.

Stegosaurus was not the brightest of dinos. It had a very small head and a brain the size of a lime.

This plant-eater's front legs were short compared to its hind legs, giving it an unusual head-down posture.

The hind feet were very broad, to support Stegosaurus's huge weight.

# STEGOSAURUS, USA

In an area now called Dinosaur Ridge in the U.S. state of Colorado about 155 million years ago, many majestic creatures roam the land. As big as a bus and armed with four 90-centimetre tail spikes, Stegosaurus is an intimidating opponent. This large plant-eater is not built for running, so it relies on its spikes to keep itself safe. One of its main enemies is Allosaurus – the top predator of the time.

And this hunter fancies his chances of grabbing some lunch. But the Stegosaurus stands his ground, whipping his deadly tail from side to side. In a threatening display, he flushes blood into the plates along his back to warn off the attacker. The Allosaurus, weighing up his options, decides he doesn't want to get too close to those tail spikes – he beats a swift retreat, hoping for easier pickings elsewhere.

With its 10-centimetre-long teeth, its strong hooked claws, and its keen sense of smell, Allosaurus was a fearsome killing machine.

The plates on Stegosaurus's back had blood vessels near the surface. The dino may have tilted them towards the sun to absorb heat and warm up.

### Stegosaurus

**Meaning:** 'Roofed lizard'
**First Fossil Found:** USA
**Date:** Late Jurassic

**Group:** Stegosaurs
**Diet:** Plants
**Size:** 9 metres long

USA

Cedar Mountain

Tenontosaurus was a plant-eating dinosaur that would have lived in herds among these forests, keeping a keen eye out for hunters.

A single Deinonychus would have been too small to bring down a Tenontosaurus alone, but a pack of these predators could work together to outwit larger creatures.

The terrifying Velociraptors in the film Jurassic Park were actually based on Deinonychus; real Velociraptors are much smaller.

Deinonychus is known for the deadly, sickle-shaped talon on the second toe of each hind foot. It probably used this for pinning down prey.

## PACK-HUNTING WITH THE
# DEINONYCHUS, USA

On a forested floodplain about 110 million years ago, in an area now called Cedar Mountain, a pack of stealthy hunters are preparing for an ambush. A lone Tenontosaurus has been separated from her herd. She stops for a drink, unaware of the hunters around her. All at once, the pack of Deinonychus burst from the shadows, flinging themselves at their prey.

The Tenontosaurus is much bigger than her attackers, but they have strength in numbers. Two of the hunters leap up on the back of the lumbering plant-eater, digging in with their sickle-shaped talons to hold on. They pin down their docile prey, ripping into her with their vicious teeth. Meanwhile, the other members of the pack crowd around, closing in for the kill.

This bone-crunching meat-eater probably had a bite similar in strength to a modern-day alligator. Its jaws were crammed with 70 bladelike teeth.

It is likely that this nimble hunter was covered in feathers. In fact, Deinonychus and other similar dinosaurs were close relatives of today's birds!

The agile Deinonychus used its long tail to keep it balanced while running and turning.

This slithering creature, named Coniophis, was one of the world's first ever snakes.

**Deinonychus**

**Meaning:** 'Terrible claw'
**First Fossil Found:** USA
**Date:** Early Cretaceous

**Group:** Theropods
**Diet:** Meat
**Size:** 3 metres long

USA

New Mexico

The claws of Nothronychus would have measured up to 30 centimetres long. Ouch!

Why was Nothronychus pot-bellied? Because it ate so many plants, its stomach had to work extra-hard to digest everything, making it large and bulging.

Nothronychus had a coat of shaggy feathers, rather like a modern-day emu.

Nothronychus belonged to a group of dinosaurs called the therizinosaurs. They were very rare in North America, so Nothronychus would have been an unusual sight.

This coelurosaur was a small hunter, who would have eaten lizards and mammals. It may even have ganged up with others to bring down larger prey.

Don't let the claws fool you. Despite its frightening talons, this bizarre-looking creature was not a fearsome meat-eater, but a vegetarian! This dinosaur was a close relative of carnivores such as Tyrannosaurus rex. At some point, creatures like this would have eaten meat but, as they evolved, they became plant-eaters, perhaps so as not to compete with other meat-eaters in the area.

Nothronychus walked on two legs, using its long neck to reach high into the trees for food to eat. It would have used its huge claws to drag branches towards it, so it could feast on the leaves. This pot-bellied creature was not the most elegant mover, waddling on its stout legs. And neither was it particularly fast, so it would have relied on its fierce-looking claws to scare off attackers.

Herds of Zuniceratops would have roamed these forests, stripping vegetation from plants with their strong mouths.

Nothronychus was the equivalent of a modern-day panda – which also evolved from meat-eaters, but eats only plants.

The first Zuniceratops fossil was discovered by an eight-year-old boy. This horned dinosaur was related to Triceratops, but lived millions of years before it.

**Nothronychus**
**Meaning:** 'Slothful claw'
**First Fossil Found:** USA
**Date:** Mid Cretaceous
**Group:** Therizinosaurs
**Diet:** Plants
**Size:** 5 metres long

**LOCKING HORNS WITH THE**

# TRICERATOPS, USA

Sixty-eight million years ago, on a wide floodplain known as Hell Creek, a mighty battle is about to begin. Two rival male Triceratops are squaring up, each eager to prove that he is the strongest in the herd. At first, they keep their distance, swinging their vast heads from side to side in a threatening display. Their bony head crests flush with blood as they try to intimidate each other. Then, as neither male wants to back down, they come together with a furious crash, grunting and bellowing. Like rutting stags, they lock horns, each trying to stand his ground. At last, there is a sickening crunch – the weaker dinosaur has snapped a horn, and the battle is over. The wounded loser retreats to the forest, while the victor surveys his herd in triumph.

When trying to impress the ladies, a male Triceratops would lower his head to show off his neck frill.

This plant-eater had one of the most powerful mouths of any animal ever – it could slice through tree trunks with its sharp beak, grinding them to a pulp with its massive teeth.

A frill of solid bone protected the Triceratops' soft neck.

The horns above a Triceratops' eyes could grow up to a metre long!

Triceratops' eyes were set wide apart so it could look around for predators, including the fearsome T. rex.

This plodding dino was a slow mover – it couldn't run away from predators, so it had to rely on its horns for defence.

Pterosaurs patrolled the Late Cretaceous skies.

Hell Creek

USA

In the waters of Hell Creek lurked deadly crocodiles, like this Brachychampsa.

Turtles such as Adocus would have had to stay on their guard to avoid predators looking for an easy meal.

This dinosaur's huge head made up a third of its total length.

How do we know that Triceratops used to fight each other? Because dinosaur experts have found old horn wounds near the eye sockets and on the neck frills of fossils.

### Triceratops

**Meaning:** 'Three-horned face'  **Group:** Ceratopsids
**First Fossil Found:** USA  **Diet:** Plants
**Date:** Late Cretaceous  **Size:** 9 metres long

CANADA
Alberta
Saskatchewan

Torosaurus was a cousin of Triceratops. It had one of the largest skulls of any land animal ever, measuring nearly 3 metres long.

The armoured Ankylosaurus had a massive bony club on the end of its tail – just the right height for smashing into a T. rex's knee!

As well as hunting live prey, T. rex may have scavenged for dead animals.

Herds of Edmontosaurus may have made a round-trip of 2,600 kilometres each year to reach the best feeding grounds.

STALKING PREY WITH THE

# TYRANNOSAURUS, CANADA

The far north of Alaska 67 million years ago received very little sunlight during the freezing winter months, just like today. As the Arctic winter began, large herds of dinosaurs – such as Edmontosaurus – would have set off to travel hundreds of kilometres south, towards warmer lands with more plentiful food. Many Edmontosaurus fossils have been found both in Alaska and at the other end of the migratory route, in the southern Canadian provinces of Alberta and Saskatchewan.

This herd of Edmontosaurus have nearly reached the end of their epic journey, but they are not out of danger yet. As volcanoes spew ash across the landscape, the herd prepares to pass through a narrow canyon. But they are not alone – for the last few miles they have been shadowed by one of the mightiest hunters ever to roam the planet: the deadly Tyrannosaurus rex. As the plant-eaters funnel into the canyon, the T. rex takes his chance and strikes, seizing a straggler who can put up little defence.

This deadly predator had an enormous skull, 1.5 metres long!

After catching its prey, T. rex would rip off chunks of flesh and bone. Its bite was so strong that it could crunch up bones along with the meat.

This mighty hunter was twice as tall as an elephant and had a 4-metre-long stride. It had a top running speed of 32 kilometres per hour.

The massive droppings of T. rex were as long as a human arm and weighed the same as a 6-month-old baby!

Edmontosaurus was a large, plant-eating dinosaur from the duck-billed family. It measured up to 12 metres long, making it a hearty meal for a hunter.

**Tyrannosaurus**

**Meaning:** 'Tyrant lizard'  
**First Fossil Found:** USA  
**Date:** Late Cretaceous

**Group:** Tyrannosaurs  
**Diet:** Meat  
**Size:** 12 metres long

USA

Kansas

To walk on land, many pterosaurs used their folded wings as front legs.

It's likely that many pterosaurs took to the air by vaulting on their wing bones, like pole-vaulters!

Adult male Pteranodons had brightly coloured head crests, probably for attracting females.

Some pterosaurs had long necks with throat pouches like a pelican's, for storing fish.

Because young pterosaurs were much smaller and lighter than the adults, it may have been easier for them to get airborne.

Pterosaur hatchlings looked like tiny versions of the adults — they would have been able to look after themselves from a very young age.

# LEARNING TO FLY WITH THE
# BABY PTERANODON, USA

On a rugged clifftop beside an enormous ocean, a young Pteranodon is about to take her first flight. Eighty-five million years ago, a huge ocean covered much of what is now the USA. The skies above this ocean were ruled by a group of winged reptiles called the pterosaurs. These cousins of the dinosaurs are the largest flying animals ever to have existed: some were the size of small planes!

These little Pteranodons hatched only a few days ago. The mothers left after burying their eggs, leaving the chicks to fend for themselves. The youngsters know that they must take flight in search of food. Each shuffles towards the cliff edge, peering down at the crashing waves below. Copying those around her, a chick crouches down, vaults forward on folded wings and launches herself into the air. Phew!

Adult Pteranodons had such wide wingspans that once they were airborne, they didn't need to flap much, but could just soar on air currents, like a modern-day albatross.

This type of Pteranodon was enormous, with a wingspan as wide as 7 metres!

Pterosaurs had hollow bones, like birds, which made them very light. Their wings were made from a thin membrane of leathery skin supported by an elongated fourth finger bone.

A furry body kept a pterosaur warm, like the feathers of a modern-day bird.

### Pteranodon

**Meaning:** 'Toothless wing'
**First Fossil Found:** USA
**Date:** Late Cretaceous
**Group:** Pterosaurs
**Diet:** Fish
**Size:** 7-metre wingspan

USA

South Dakota

Nyctosaurus was a pterosaur with a huge crest on its head, probably for display.

Just like modern sea turtles, Archelon laid its eggs by burying them at night-time on a beach.

Dolichorhynchops was a plesiosaur that grew up to 5 metres long. It hunted fish, swallowing them whole.

Measuring up to 11 metres, Tylosaurus — a type of mosasaur — was a powerful predator that may have hunted Archelon.

As well as its bony shell, Archelon had four tough plates on its belly, protecting it from attacks from below.

Archelon's oarlike flippers helped to propel it through the waters.

This 5-metre-long fish, called Xiphactinus, patrolled the Late Cretaceous seas, scooping up fish and seabirds in its monstrous jaws.

This giant sea turtle may have lived for over 100 years!

## CRUISING WITH THE

# ARCHELON, USA

One of the largest sea turtles ever to have roamed the oceans was Archelon. This creature was the size of a small car, weighing nearly as much as an elephant. It cruised the shallow sea that covered much of North America 80 million years ago. Archelon had an enormous head, measuring up to a metre long, with a sharp beak. It used this to guzzle up squid and jellyfish that it found floating near the water's surface.

This ancient ocean was packed with predators, so Archelon had to be on its guard. Although it was big, its predators were even bigger: Archelon was hunted by huge marine reptiles called mosasaurs, as well as by sharks and crocodiles. Although Archelon had a protective shell, it couldn't withdraw its head or flippers inside this shell, so it was a target for hunters. These waters were a dangerous place to be!

Mosasaurs and plesiosaurs were distant relatives of the dinosaurs. These marine reptiles couldn't breathe underwater, so they had to poke their heads above the surface now and then for air.

This flightless bird, called Hesperornis, swam in the sea like a penguin. It would have made easy pickings for the deadly marine monsters that prowled these waters.

Elasmosaurus was another type of plesiosaur, measuring 14 metres long. Its super-long neck would have allowed it to scoop up shellfish from the sea floor.

**Archelon**

**Meaning:** 'Ruling turtle'
**First Fossil Found:** USA
**Date:** Late Cretaceous

**Group:** Protostegids
**Diet:** Omnivore
**Size:** 4 metres long

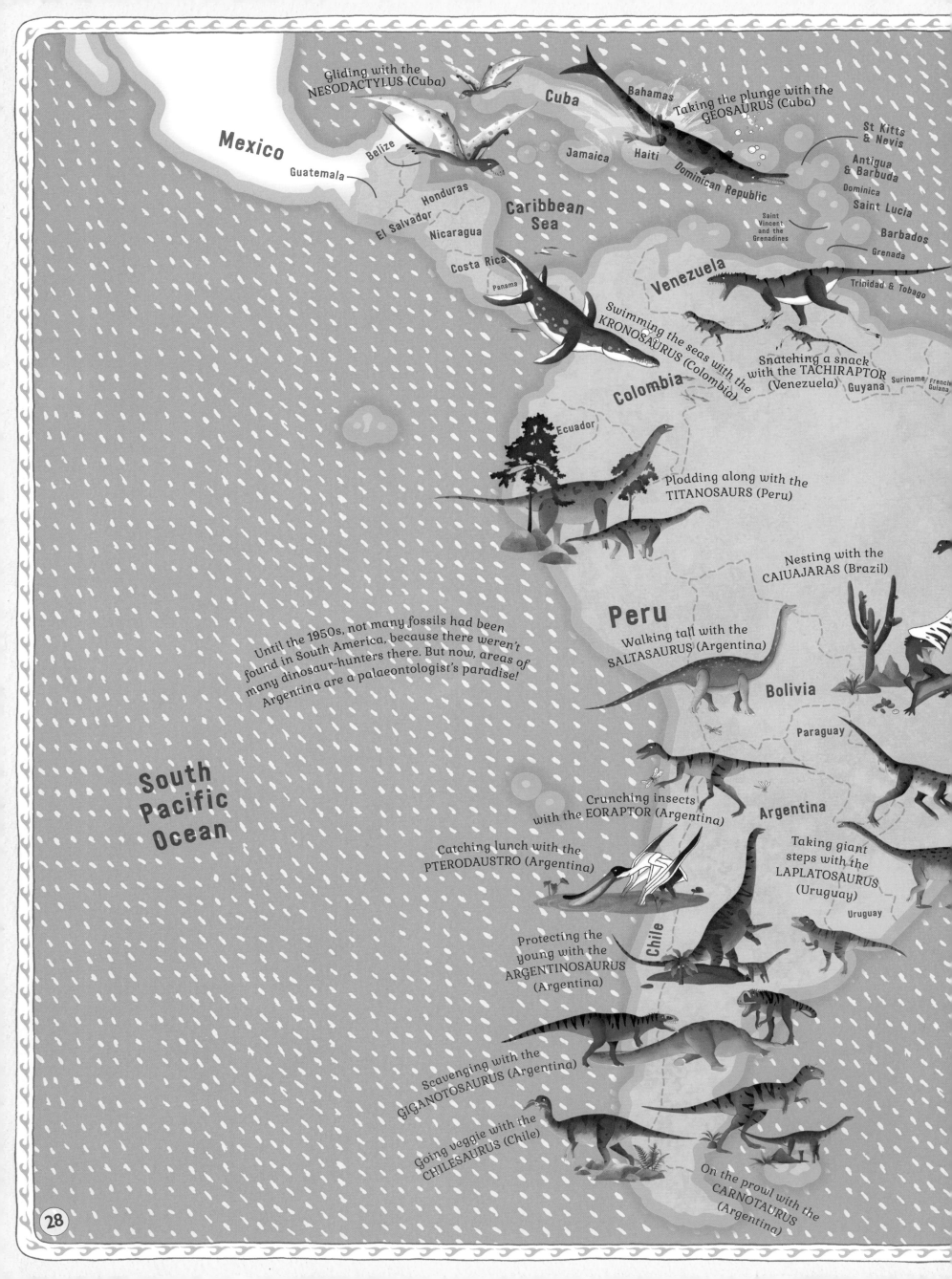

Gliding with the
NESODACTYLUS (Cuba)

Taking the plunge with the
GEOSAURUS (Cuba)

**Cuba**

Bahamas

Mexico

Belize

Guatemala

Jamaica

Haiti

Dominican Republic

St Kitts
& Nevis

Antigua
& Barbuda

Dominica

Saint Lucia

Saint
Vincent
and the
Grenadines

Barbados

Grenada

Honduras

El Salvador

Nicaragua

**Caribbean
Sea**

Costa Rica

Panama

Swimming the seas with the
KRONOSAURUS (Colombia)

**Venezuela**

Trinidad & Tobago

Snatching a snack
with the TACHIRAPTOR
(Venezuela)

Guyana

Suriname

French
Guiana

**Colombia**

Ecuador

Plodding along with the
TITANOSAURS (Peru)

Nesting with the
CAIUAJARAS (Brazil)

**Peru**

Until the 1950s, not many fossils had been
found in South America, because there weren't
many dinosaur-hunters there. But now, areas of
Argentina are a palaeontologist's paradise!

Walking tall with the
SALTASAURUS (Argentina)

**Bolivia**

Paraguay

**South
Pacific
Ocean**

Crunching insects
with the EORAPTOR (Argentina)

**Argentina**

Catching lunch with the
PTERODAUSTRO (Argentina)

Taking giant
steps with the
LAPLATOSAURUS
(Uruguay)

Uruguay

Chile

Protecting the
young with the
ARGENTINOSAURUS
(Argentina)

Scavenging with the
GIGANOTOSAURUS (Argentina)

Going veggie with the
CHILESAURUS (Chile)

On the prowl with the
CARNOTAURUS
(Argentina)

# CENTRAL & SOUTH AMERICA

South America was home to the giants of the dinosaur world: more long-necked titanosaurs have been discovered here than on any other continent. In 2014, experts in Argentina unearthed a 40-metre-long dinosaur: the largest land animal ever discovered! This region is also home to some of the oldest dinosaur fossils ever found, including the tiny hunter Eoraptor.

Fishing for supper with the IRRITATOR (Brazil)

Dwarfing your neighbours with the GONDWANATITAN (Brazil)

Darting with the STAURIKOSAURUS (Brazil)

## South Atlantic Ocean

For much of the age of dinosaurs, South America was connected to Africa. Fossils of some types of dinosaur – such as the spinosaurs – have been found on both continents.

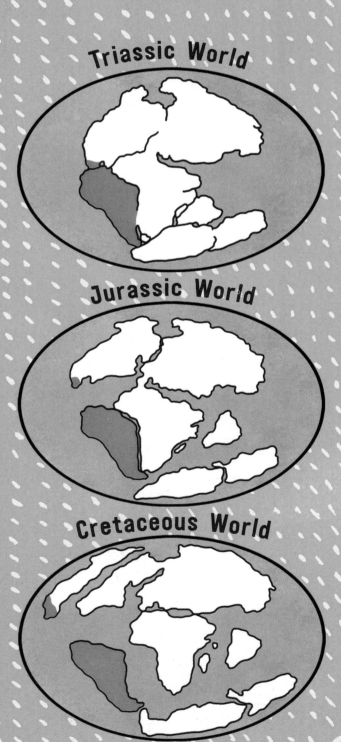

Triassic World

Jurassic World

Cretaceous World

San Luis
Province

ARGENTINA

Hatchlings grew quickly: within two years
these babies would have reached
half their adult size.

These winged reptiles may have
swallowed stones to help grind the
food inside their stomachs!

This creature's large, splayed hind feet
would have helped keep it balanced when
feeding, and might even have helped it swim.

Pterodaustro's bizarre curved bill contained
about 1,000 teeth. The lower teeth sieved food
from the water, which was then crunched
up by the small, blunt upper teeth.

Pterodaustro might have been nocturnal – maybe because its food was more plentiful at night, or maybe to avoid predators that prowled by day.

**Pterodaustro**

**Meaning:** 'Southern wing'
**First Fossil Found:** Argentina
**Date:** Early Cretaceous
**Group:** Pterosaurs
**Diet:** Omnivore
**Size:** 2-metre wingspan

Pterodaustro parents would have stayed with their eggs, instead of burying them and leaving them like some other pterosaurs.

Some experts think that, like flamingos, Pterodaustro may have had a pink colour because of all the pink shrimps they ate. But others think this is unlikely!

With a long body and neck, Pterodaustro may have found taking off tricky, needing a bit of a run up and a lot of flapping.

**CATCHING LUNCH WITH THE**

# PTERODAUSTRO, ARGENTINA

About 105 million years ago, if you stopped by a large, salty inland lake in what is now Argentina, you might have seen an extraordinary sight. Just as flamingos flock to feed in their thousands today, so might a creature called Pterodaustro have gathered in huge numbers way back then. Pterodaustro was a type of winged reptile called a pterosaur. To feed, it stood in shallow lakes, scooping up mouthfuls of water with its long, upward-curving beak.

Its lower jaws were lined with hundreds of long, bristle-like teeth, which were designed to sieve tiny shrimp and plankton from the water. Pterodaustro fed and nested in large groups: parents would have taken care of their eggs and hatchlings, unlike some other species of pterosaur. This salty lake was not a hospitable place for most creatures to survive, but it was just right for Pterodaustro. Peckish for plankton? Well, grab yourself a sieve – grub's up!

Argentinosaurus had interlocking bones along its spine, making a bone bridge to support its weight.

Packs of Mapusaurus mobbed herds of large plant-eaters, tearing off chunks of meat as they sped past. Fast food indeed!

Neuquén Province

ARGENTINA

## PROTECTING THE YOUNG WITH THE
# ARGENTINOSAURUS, ARGENTINA

The biggest animals ever to have walked the Earth were a group of sauropod dinosaurs called the titanosaurs. And one of the largest of these was an enormous creature called Argentinosaurus. This plant-eater roamed the plains and forests of South America 95 million years ago. These giants needed to eat up to 100 kilograms of plants every single day to gain enough energy just to keep going. This meant that herds of Argentinosaurus were always on the move, covering hundreds of kilometres in search of new land on which to graze.

As this herd plods along, danger is never far away. The adults keep the youngsters in the middle of the herd, out of harm's way. But they are shadowed by a gang of hungry Mapusaurus, eager for meat. The speedy Mapusaurus dart in and out between the lumbering sauropods. Soon, they have separated a youngster from the rest of the herd. But before they can strike, one of the giants rears up on her hind legs with a bellowing cry. She thunders to the ground, her huge feet narrowly missing the startled hunters, who scatter and slink away. The youngster is safe... for now.

An adult Argentinosaurus was the same height as a five-storey building, and weighed as much as 75 tonnes: that's the same as 15 African elephants!

The incredibly long neck of this giant dino meant that it could stand in one spot and feed on plants all around without moving its legs, saving its energy.

This giant was covered in bony lumps of skin, some the size of a fist, to protect it from the piercing teeth of predators.

The extremely strong, flexible tail of Argentinosaurus was used for balance when the dino reared up on its hind legs.

Argentinosaurus was a slow mover, with a top speed of only 8 kilometres per hour. Mapusaurus, on the other hand, could reach speeds of 48 kilometres per hour.

Mapusaurus was a fierce predator about the same size as a Tyrannosaurus rex, but with a less powerful bite.

Titanosaurs didn't stop growing throughout their lives.

In 1988, a South American sheep farmer found an old tree trunk on his farm... it turned out to be the fossilised leg bone of Argentinosaurus!

**Argentinosaurus**

**Meaning:** 'Argentina lizard'
**First Fossil Found:** Argentina
**Date:** Late Cretaceous

**Group:** Sauropods
**Diet:** Plants
**Size:** 35 metres long

ARGENTINA

Patagonia

Experts think that Giganotosaurus could run at speeds of up to 35 kilometres per hour.

Andesaurus was a titanosaur with a length of about 16 metres — that's the same as one and a half double-decker buses!

This dino's skull was a whopping 2 metres long — bigger than the skull of the mighty T. rex. But despite this, Giganotosaurus had a smaller brain than T. rex.

Giganotosaurus had 20-centimetre-long, serrated teeth, perfect for sawing through its prey's tough skin.

Powerful neck muscles helped Giganotosaurus tear off chunks of meat larger than a human!

# GIGANOTOSAURUS, ARGENTINA

Ninety-seven million years ago in what is now southern Argentina, a mighty dinosaur named Giganotosaurus was the top hunter. This creature was one of the largest meat-eaters ever to have lived, larger even than Tyrannosaurus rex, who dominated North America! But even top hunters need an extra snack at times, so as well as killing prey, Giganotosaurus was not beyond scavenging meat from creatures that were already dead.

This pack of Giganotosaurus have come across the remains of a huge sauropod called Andesaurus. The massive body of this plodding plant-eater has triggered a feeding frenzy, with many creatures flocking for a feast. But as the pack of deadly Giganotosaurus approaches, the smaller animals flee, not keen on a confrontation. The group rip into the carcass with steak-knife teeth, leaving the other hungry scavengers looking on helplessly.

Giganotosaurus's long, muscular tail helped it balance and turn quickly when running.

This fierce dinosaur brought down its victims using powerful, slicing bites.

The long legs of this huge hunter meant that it could outrun any plant-eater.

This land-based crocodile, called Araripesuchus, may have raided the nests of dinosaurs, gobbling up the hatchlings.

Buitreraptor was a small meat-eater who snatched up lizards and mammals with its sharp, hooked teeth.

**Gigantosaurus**

**Meaning:** 'Giant southern lizard'
**First Fossil Found:** Argentina
**Date:** Late Cretaceous

**Group:** Theropods
**Diet:** Meat
**Size:** 14 metres long

## Caiuajaras

**Meaning:** 'Pterosaur from Caiuá'
**First Fossil Found:** Brazil
**Date:** Late Cretaceous
**Group:** Pterosaurs
**Diet:** Plants
**Size:** 2.35-metre wingspan

The Caiuajaras were fairly small pterosaurs: the largest had wingspans measuring just over 2 metres – similar in size to a modern-day albatross.

This ancient species of iguana roamed the Late Cretaceous deserts.

Experts think that Caiuajaras likely fed on fruit, playing an important role in spreading the seeds of flowering plants, just like birds do today.

### NESTING WITH THE
# CAIUAJARAS, BRAZIL

Not many creatures could survive in the middle of a desert, but a group of pterosaurs – the Caiuajaras – have chosen this spot as their home. Amid the sand dunes of what is now southern Brazil, about 80 million years ago, these strange-looking creatures live in a huge colony. Gathering around a lake oasis, they squawk, squabble and shriek as they pick out their mates and the best sites for nesting. They strut and preen, showing off their enormous head crests to attract attention. The females lay their eggs then bury them in the sand. Soon after the youngsters hatch, they are ready for their first flight, taking to the skies and soaring over the wide landscape in search of fruits to eat. Out in the harsh desert, these creatures don't have many predators to worry about. The main danger is the threat of violent dust storms, which is never far away.

These creatures had enormous sail-shaped head crests, which got larger as they grew. They probably used them for display.

BRAZIL

Paraná State

Caiuajaras were social animals, living in groups with lots of others.

Young Caiuajaras looked like miniature adults — they would have fended for themselves soon after hatching.

In the 1970s, a farmer and his son discovered a huge bone bed in southern Brazil, containing the remains of dozens of Caiuajaras.

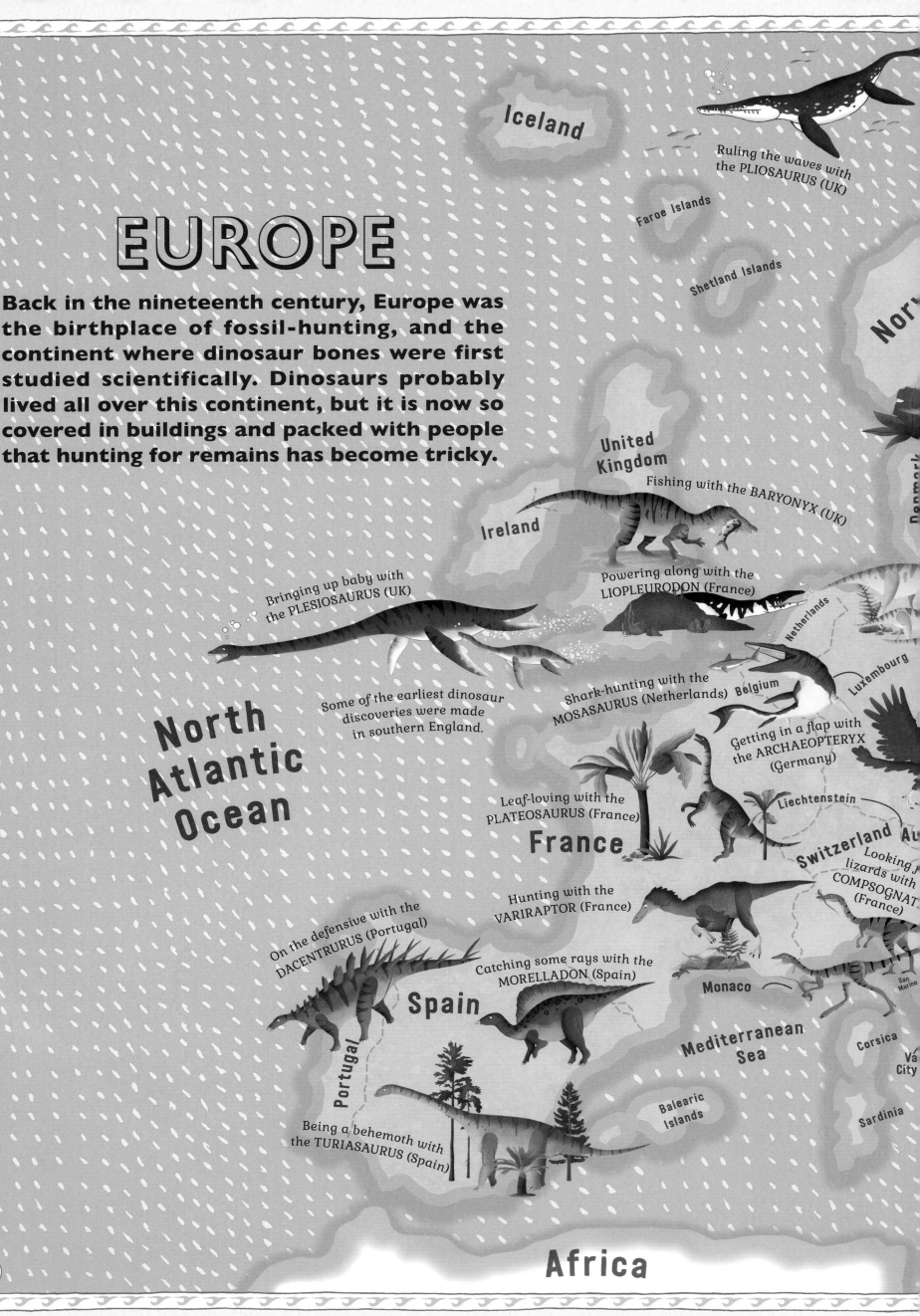

# EUROPE

Back in the nineteenth century, Europe was the birthplace of fossil-hunting, and the continent where dinosaur bones were first studied scientifically. Dinosaurs probably lived all over this continent, but it is now so covered in buildings and packed with people that hunting for remains has become tricky.

Iceland

Ruling the waves with the PLIOSAURUS (UK)

Faroe Islands

Shetland Islands

Nor

United Kingdom

Fishing with the BARYONYX (UK)

Ireland

Powering along with the LIOPLEURODON (France)

Den

Bringing up baby with the PLESIOSAURUS (UK)

Netherlands

Luxembourg

Shark-hunting with the MOSASAURUS (Netherlands)  Belgium

Some of the earliest dinosaur discoveries were made in southern England.

## North Atlantic Ocean

Getting in a flap with the ARCHAEOPTERYX (Germany)

Leaf-loving with the PLATEOSAURUS (France)

Liechtenstein

France

Switzerland  Au

Looking
lizards with
COMPSOGNAT
(France)

Hunting with the VARIRAPTOR (France)

On the defensive with the DACENTRURUS (Portugal)

Catching some rays with the MORELLADON (Spain)

San Marino

Monaco

Spain

Mediterranean Sea

Corsica

Va
City

Portugal

Balearic Islands

Sardinia

Being a behemoth with the TURIASAURUS (Spain)

Africa

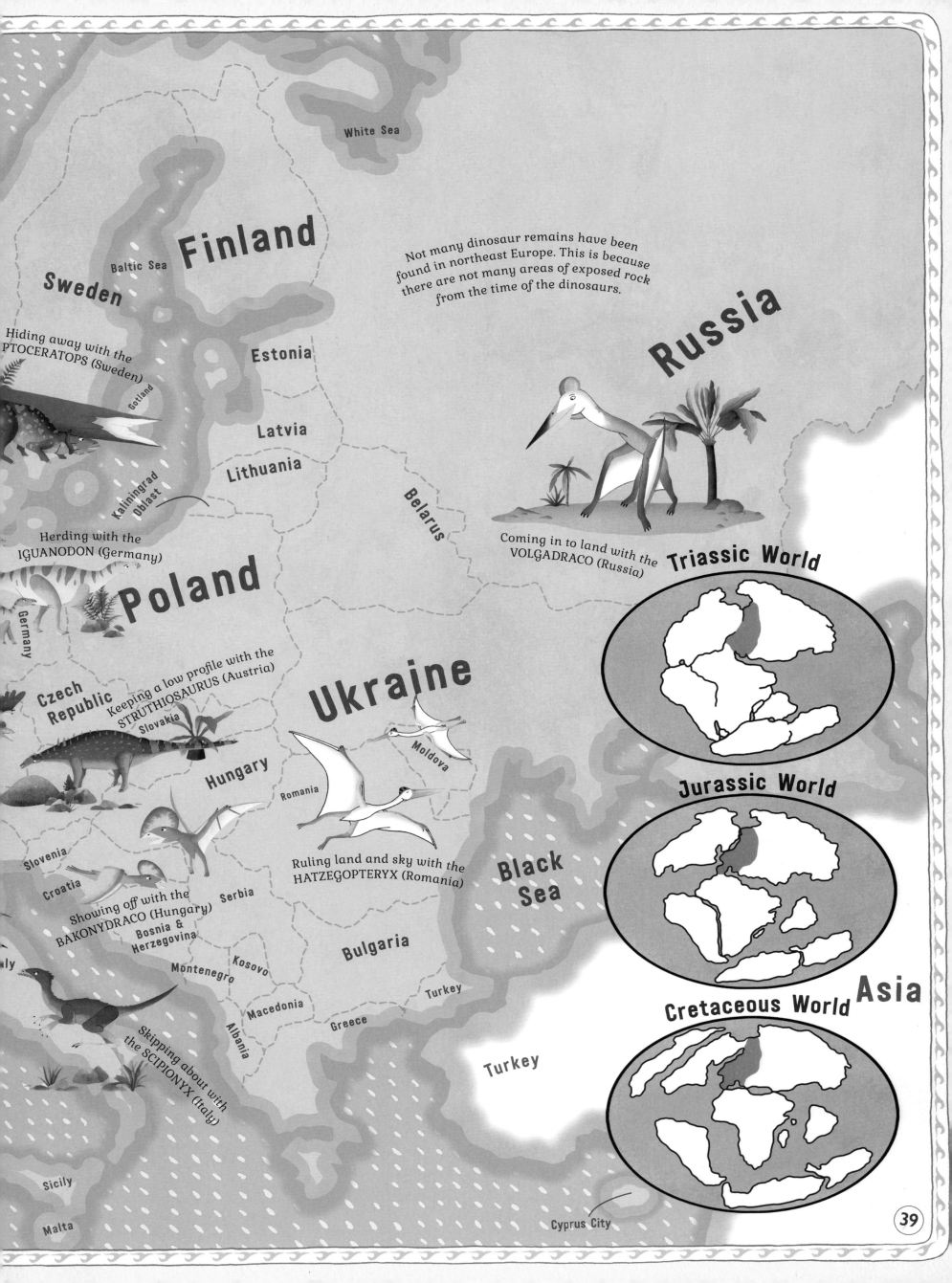

White Sea

Finland

Baltic Sea

Sweden

Not many dinosaur remains have been found in northeast Europe. This is because there are not many areas of exposed rock from the time of the dinosaurs.

Russia

Hiding away with the
PTOCERATOPS (Sweden)

Estonia

Latvia

Lithuania

Belarus

Coming in to land with the
VOLGADRACO (Russia)

Triassic World

Herding with the
IGUANODON (Germany)

Poland

Czech
Republic

Keeping a low profile with the
STRUTHIOSAURUS (Austria)

Slovakia

Hungary

Ukraine

Moldova

Romania

Jurassic World

Slovenia

Croatia

Showing off with the
BAKONYDRACO (Hungary)

Bosnia &
Herzegovina

Serbia

Ruling land and sky with the
HATZEGOPTERYX (Romania)

Black
Sea

Montenegro

Kosovo

Bulgaria

Macedonia

Turkey

Albania

Greece

Turkey

Cretaceous World

Asia

Skipping about with
the SCIPIONYX (Italy)

Sicily

Malta

Cyprus City

39

UNITED
KINGDOM

Dorset

To steer, Plesiosaurus used both its long
neck – like a rudder – and its front flippers.

This reptile had about 50 sharply
pointed teeth, which helped it snatch
fish from the water.

Measuring up to 20 metres long, Liopleurodon was the top predator
in these waters. It had massive jaws lined with deadly teeth.

A Plesiosaurus fed on fish and squidlike
creatures, and also scooped up shellfish from
the sea floor. It swallowed stones to help grind
up food inside its stomach.

## BRINGING UP BABY WITH THE
# PLESIOSAURUS, UK

During the Jurassic period, about 190
million years ago, Europe was covered
by a warm, shallow sea, bursting with
life. In these balmy waters lived a
distant relative of the dinosaurs called
Plesiosaurus. This mother Plesiosaurus
has recently given birth to her baby. She
has only one calf, so all of her efforts are
devoted to protecting it. In the time
they have together, she must teach the
youngster all it needs to know to survive
in these dangerous seas.

The pair bask close to the sea surface,
sometimes poking their heads above the
water to take a breath of air. The calf
stays near its mother, sheltering next to
her body to stay out of sight of deadly
predators, such as the huge Liopleurodon.
From the corner of her eye the mother
glimpses the shape of a Liopleurodon
passing below. She tenses, moving closer
to her youngster, both of them ready to
flee. But the monster cruises on, not
interested in grabbing a meal just now.

Ichthyosaurs were strong
swimmers who moved through
the water by swishing their tails
from side to side, like sharks.

The first Plesiosaurus fossil was discovered by an eminent fossil-hunter called Mary Anning, in Dorset in 1823. This was one of the earliest prehistoric creatures to be discovered, and caused much excitement in Victorian England.

A mother Plesiosaurus would have defended her baby from attackers, delivering a sharp slap with a flipper to any sharks or other hunters that came too close.

These creatures had large lungs, meaning they could stay underwater for long spells before having to surface for air.

Plesiosaurus used its large, muscular flippers to propel itself through the water, like a modern-day penguin.

To gather stones and shellfish, Plesiosaurus may have ploughed with its snout along the sea bed.

**Plesiosaurus**

**Meaning:** 'Near-lizard'
**First Fossil Found:** UK
**Date:** Early Jurassic

**Group:** Plesiosaurs
**Diet:** Fish and meat
**Size:** 3.5 metres long

Iguanodon was a plant-eater who lived in herds, grazing on ferns. It had a sharp thumb spike, which it used to defend itself.

The top hunter in these parts was Neovenator. Related to Allosaurus, this fierce predator probably hunted Iguanodons.

Baryonyx spent much of its time in the water, but it may also have scavenged for other food on land.

Baryonyx had powerful arms and large hands for seizing prey.

Baryonyx's skull was shaped like a crocodile's. It used its long jaws to snatch fish from the water. These jaws were angled to stop fish from wriggling away.

## FISHING WITH THE
# BARYONYX, UK

The south of Britain 125 million years ago was a lush floodplain dotted with woodland and criss-crossed by rivers. In the marshes here lived an unusual dinosaur: Baryonyx. This dinosaur was a predator but – unlike many of its relatives – it didn't hunt on land. Its domain was the water.

This pair of Baryonyx are doing a spot of fishing. They stand in the shallow river, their quick eyes scanning the surface for signs of lunch.

A silvery flash reveals a fish passing by beneath. One of the hunters snatches at the fish, spearing it with a deadly talon and then tossing it between his long jaws. Just like today's crocodiles, Baryonyx's mouth is perfectly formed for holding on to slippery fish. He tilts his head back and then swallows – gulp – guzzling down his victim all in one. Then he crouches in the river again, motionless, with his eyes glued to the water, looking out for seconds.

UNITED KINGDOM

Surrey

This fish-eater had 64 teeth, which were long, pointed and finely serrated — making a perfect fish snare.

For larger prey, Baryonyx used its 35-centimetre-long claw like a spear.

Baryonyx was the first fish-eating dino ever discovered. An amateur fossil-hunter found its huge talon in a clay pit in Surrey in 1983.

How do we know that Baryonyx ate fish? Because experts have found the fossilised remains of fish scales in its stomach!

**Baryonyx**

**Meaning:** 'Heavy claw'
**First Fossil Found:** UK
**Date:** Early Cretaceous
**Group:** Theropods
**Diet:** Fish and meat
**Size:** 7.5 metres long

# MOSASAURUS, NETHERLANDS

These days, sharks are the ocean's top predators. But 70 million years ago, it was a different story. During the Late Cretaceous period, 80 per cent of the planet was covered in water, and these seas were a brutal place to live. The oceans were ruled by an enormous killing-machine called Mosasaurus. The size of a bus, Mosasaurus could power through the water using its huge, muscular tail, and could swallow prey whole.

This predator was at the very top of the food chain: even deadly sharks were on the menu. The Squalicorax shark was similar in size to a modern-day great white shark, but would have been no match for a large Mosasaurus. Mosasaurus would have hunted its prey using an ambush technique – lurking near the sea floor until its victim drew near, then charging towards it at speeds of up to 50 kilometres per hour. Crunch, crunch, shark for lunch!

The super-strength hearing of Mosasaurus would have helped it pinpoint prey in the vast seas.

Squalicorax was a type of shark that would have been common in the Cretaceous seas.

This mighty predator dominated the planet. In fact, mosasaur bones have been found on every continent in the world — including Antarctica!

The first Mosasaurus remains ever discovered were unearthed near the Meuse River in the Netherlands in 1764.

NETHERLANDS

Meuse River

44

Mosasaurus had a flexible skull and a double-hinged jaw, like a modern-day snake's, meaning that it could swallow its prey whole.

This hunter was built for killing: it had a second set of deadly teeth on the roof of its mouth, perfect for pinning down prey.

Mosasaurus could spend long hours under the water before needing to come up for air.

As long as a bus and weighing about the same as two African elephants, Mosasaurus was an enormous beast.

The long tail of Mosasaurus was flattened like a modern-day alligator's. The creature used this tail to propel itself along, steering with its paddles.

**Mosasaurus**

**Meaning:** 'Meuse River lizard'
**First Fossil Found:** Netherlands
**Date:** Late Cretaceous

**Group:** Mosasaurs
**Diet:** Fish and Meat
**Size:** 15 metres long

## RULING LAND AND SKY WITH THE
# HATZEGOPTERYX, ROMANIA

The island of Hateg 66 million years ago was home to some extraordinary creatures. Because this island – which is now part of Romania – was cut off from other places, food was in short supply. This meant that many of its dinosaurs were tiny in comparison to their relations on the mainland. But, as well as being home to some dwarfish dinos, Hateg was also the home of the largest flying animal ever known: the enormous Hatzegopteryx.

Hatzegopteryx was a monstrous pterosaur. It grew as tall as a giraffe with a wingspan as long as a bus. This winged giant could cruise from island to island in search of food, and it had no predators in the area, so it lived long enough to grow to a huge size. Hatzegopteryx not only ruled the skies, but also dominated on land. It could swoop down among a herd of small sauropods, snatch up a youngster and swallow it whole. Gulp!

Hatzegopteryx was the largest known pterosaur and the largest known creature ever to take to the skies.

The skull of Hatzegopteryx was about 3 metres long, which is as big as a male polar bear.

This small hadrosaur, called Telmatosaurus, browsed the plant life, munching leaves and branches.

Hatzegopteryx hunted on the ground, walking on all fours and scooping up prey in its huge beak.

**Hatzegopteryx**

**Meaning:** 'Monstrous wing of Hateg'
**First Fossil Found:** Romania
**Date:** Late Cretaceous
**Group:** Pterosaurs
**Diet:** Meat
**Size:** 11-metre wingspan

Large pterosaurs such as this may have had a top flight speed of up to 100 kilometres per hour!

These giant pterosaurs had long, sharp beaks, which they may have used as weapons when fighting with rivals.

Although it was big, Hatzegopteryx was light enough to get airborne because its bones were full of air pockets.

Transylvania

ROMANIA

Bradycneme was a small meat-eating dinosaur. When its leg bone was first discovered, scientists believed it was a 2-metre-tall owl!

Magyarosaurus was a dwarf sauropod the height of a pony. It was tiny compared with its giant cousins — weighing 70 times less than Argentinosaurus.

# AFRICA

This huge continent has revealed some incredible dinosaur finds: from the enormous Jurassic bone beds of Tanzania to the exciting new discoveries of the North African desert, which was once a lush tropical paradise, home to fish-guzzling dinosaurs, giant crocodiles and massive plant-eaters.

Running with the DELTADROMEUS (Morocco)

Madeira

Keeping cool with the CHEBSAURUS (Algeria)

Canary Islands

Morocco

Western Sahara

Mauritania

Sizing up sauropods with the CARCHARODONTOSAURUS (Algeria)

Mali

Cape Verde

Senegal

The Gambia

Guinea-Bissau

Guinea

Burkina Faso

Sierra Leone

Liberia

Ivory Coast

Ghana

Togo

**Triassic World**

**Jurassic World**

**Cretaceous World**

# North Atlantic Ocean

Ascension Island

# South Atlantic Ocean

St Helena

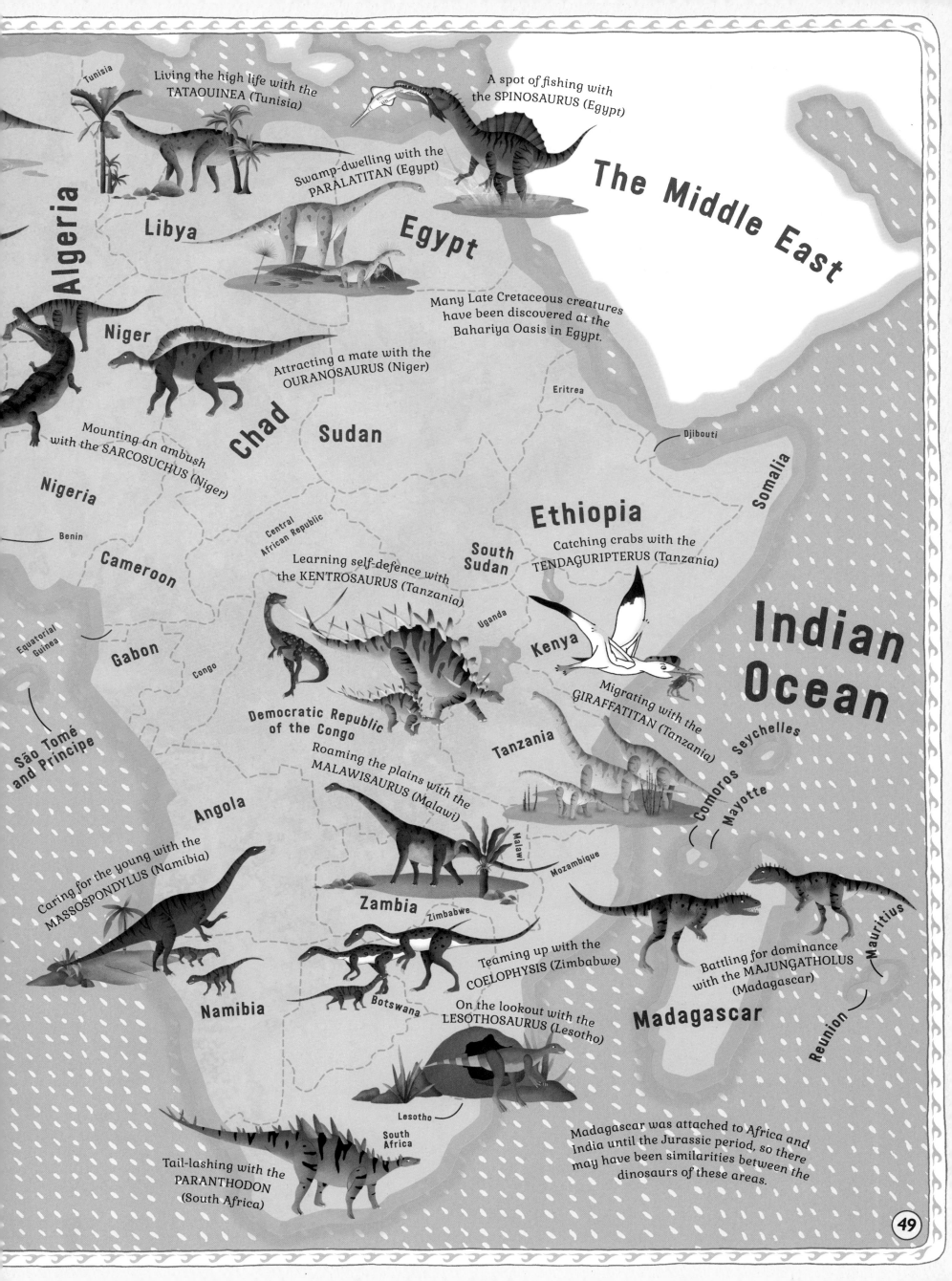

Tunisia

Living the high life with the
TATAOUINEA (Tunisia)

A spot of fishing with
the SPINOSAURUS (Egypt)

Swamp-dwelling with the
PARALATITAN (Egypt)

## Algeria

## Libya

## Egypt

# The Middle East

## Niger

Attracting a mate with the
OURANOSAURUS (Niger)

Many Late Cretaceous creatures
have been discovered at the
Bahariya Oasis in Egypt.

## Chad

## Sudan

Eritrea

Djibouti

## Somalia

Mounting an ambush
with the SARCOSUCHUS (Niger)

## Nigeria

Benin

Central
African Republic

## Ethiopia

South
Sudan

Catching crabs with the
TENDAGURIPTERUS (Tanzania)

## Cameroon

Learning self-defence with
the KENTROSAURUS (Tanzania)

Uganda

## Kenya

# Indian
# Ocean

Equatorial
Guinea

## Gabon

Congo

## Democratic Republic
## of the Congo

Migrating with the
GIRAFFATITAN (Tanzania)

## São Tomé
## and Principe

Roaming the plains with the
MALAWISAURUS (Malawi)

## Tanzania

Seychelles

Comoros

Mayotte

## Angola

Caring for the young with the
MASSOSPONDYLUS (Namibia)

Malawi

Mozambique

## Zambia

Zimbabwe

Teaming up with the
COELOPHYSIS (Zimbabwe)

Battling for dominance
with the MAJUNGATHOLUS
(Madagascar)

Mauritius

## Namibia

Botswana

On the lookout with the
LESOTHOSAURUS (Lesotho)

## Madagascar

Reunion

Tail-lashing with the
PARANTHODON
(South Africa)

Lesotho

South
Africa

Madagascar was attached to Africa and
India until the Jurassic period, so there
may have been similarities between the
dinosaurs of these areas.

Vulcanodon was an early sauropod. Unlike its giant relations who lived later, this plant-eater was only about 6 metres long.

Mashonaland West

ZIMBABWE

Since it was discovered, this dinosaur has undergone a bit of an identity crisis: first, it was named Syntarsus, then Megapnosaurus, and now Coelophysis!

This type of coelophysis, from Africa, is related to another type of coelophysis from North America.

Fossils of Coelophysis footprints show that it was a fast runner.

Coelophysis had large eyes, meaning that it would have been able to pinpoint prey among the dunes.

This lizard would have been on Coelophysis's menu. It used its speed and agility to escape from hunters.

Heterodontosaurus had three different types of teeth, which it may have used for digging up, tearing and grinding its food.

**Coelophysis**

**Meaning:** 'Hollow form'  **Group:** Theropods
**First Fossil Found:** Zimbabwe  **Diet:** Meat
**Date:** Early Jurassic  **Size:** 3 metres long

Plant-eating Massospondylus was an early relative of the giant, long-necked sauropods.

This small plant-eating dino, called Lesothosaurus, may have kept cool in the desert by burrowing underground.

The small, shrewlike Megazostrodon was an early mammal who usually hunted at night.

**TEAMING UP WITH THE**

# COELOPHYSIS, ZIMBABWE

Among the desert dunes of what is now Zimbabwe, 190 million years ago, a group of small but determined hunters are on the prowl. These dinosaurs, called Coelophysis, have tracked down a small herd of Massospondylus as they gather at a watering hole. The Coelophysis hungrily eye up one of the youngsters who has wandered away to the edge of group.

The hunters see their chance and surround the youngster from all sides, snapping and snarling. The young Massospondylus lets out a yelp of alarm, and the adults of the herd come to her aid, lashing at the predators with their sharp thumb spikes. But it is too late. The Coelophysis move fast, running on two feet – they scurry away, dragging the injured youngster with them.

51

TANZANIA

Tendaguru

This giant stood 13 metres tall and weighed as much as six elephants.

Giraffatitan's front legs were longer than its hind legs. This raised its neck and shoulders high above the ground so it could reach the treetops to feed.

Ceratosaurus fossils have been found in Africa and North America. These continents were joined together in Jurassic times.

Young sauropods had to take care when crossing the river — crocodiles lurked beneath the surface, waiting to pounce.

Giraffatitan was a close relative of the North American Brachiosaurus — in fact, it used to be called Brachiosaurus before it was renamed in 1991.

As well as leafy veg, sauropods such as Giraffatitan swallowed stones, called gastroliths, which helped break down food in the stomach.

MIGRATING WITH THE
# GIRAFFATITAN, TANZANIA

About 150 million years ago, you might have seen an impressive sight on the plains of what is now Tanzania. A herd of Giraffatitan are on the move. These massive plant-eaters are members of the sauropod family, and are some of the largest creatures to walk the Earth. As tall as a five-storey building, a Giraffatitan could graze the juiciest leaves of the treetops, which other dinosaurs couldn't

reach. Summer has arrived on the plains and the scorching temperatures mean that food is scarce and many of the waterholes have dried up. This herd of Giraffatitans is setting off on a long journey to higher ground in search of food. They will cover hundreds of kilometres, and will face many dangers on the way, from fierce predators to dangerous river crossings. But if they make it, the rewards will be worth it.

Sauropods' nostrils were high up on their heads. When these beasts were first discovered, scientists believed they lived in water and used their long necks and high nostrils as snorkels!

**Giraffatitan**

**Meaning:** 'Giant giraffe'
**First Fossil Found:** Tanzania
**Date:** Late Jurassic
**Group:** Sauropods
**Diet:** Plants
**Size:** 23 metres long

These piles of dung supported small creatures such as dung beetles, who rolled balls of dung away and laid eggs in them.

During its life, a sauropod produced several thousand tonnes of poo!

Giraffatitan would have left enormous footprints about 80 centimetres wide! These could fill with sticky mud, becoming death traps for smaller creatures.

TANZANIA

Tendaguru

Just like its cousin Stegosaurus, Kentrosaurus had small bony plates on its neck and body, like a coat of armour.

Kentrosaurus could swing its powerful spiked tail in a 180-degree arc — predators were wise to keep well clear!

Elaphrosaurus was a speedy meat-eater who prowled the Late-Jurassic plains. Its long legs and lean body helped it run fast, while its tail helped it balance and turn.

Dryosaurus was a nimble plant-eater who lived in herds and grazed on ferns.

**Kentrosaurus**

**Meaning:** 'Pointed lizard'
**First Fossil Found:** Tanzania
**Date:** Late Jurassic
**Group:** Stegosaurs
**Diet:** Plants
**Size:** 4.5 metres long

# LEARNING SELF-DEFENCE WITH THE
# KENTROSAURUS, TANZANIA

Similar to its North American cousin Stegosaurus, Kentrosaurus was a prickly customer. This very spiky stegosaur was armed with 15 pairs of deadly spikes, which it used to scare off attackers.

This mother Kentrosaurus is teaching her youngsters a lesson in self-defence. A pair of Elaphrosaurus have been sniffing around the herd for a while, seeking their chance to pick off one of the little ones. But, thanks to her excellent sense of smell,

the mother knows they are close. As the hunters approach, she rushes in front of her babies, crouching low to the ground and thrashing her tail in an arc behind her. She can swing this tail at speeds of up to 50 kilometres per hour, with such power that her deadly spikes will pierce even the thickest of hides. The hunters know when they are beaten, quickly disappearing into the undergrowth. The youngsters breathe a sigh of relief, a valuable lesson learned.

Barosaurus was a huge sauropod that measured up to 26 metres long – the length of two buses!

Kentrosaurus may have been able to rear up on its hind legs to reach tasty leaves.

As well as its 70-centimetre long tail spikes, Kentrosaurus had a long spine jutting out from each shoulder.

An ancient riverbed in Tanzania contained the bones of more than 70 different Kentrosaurus. Experts think that perhaps these dinosaurs got trapped in the mud and died.

# SARCOSUCHUS, NIGER

The Sahara Desert 112 million years ago wasn't the dry, barren place it is now, but was a tropical landscape criss-crossed by rivers. Roaming this landscape were many dinosaurs, including herds of large plant-eaters known as Nigersaurus.

A group of them have come down to the river's edge for a drink. But the river is a dangerous place to be: in the water lurks a terrifying predator. This is the king of crocodiles – Sarcosuchus. Growing as long as a bus and weighing more than a large elephant, Sarcosuchus is one of the mightiest crocodile-like reptiles that has ever lived. Just like a modern-day croc, it waits out of sight beneath the water, with only its eyes emerging above the surface. Then, when its prey draws close, it flings itself upwards, seizing its victim in its powerful jaws and dragging it to the bottom of the river to drown. This poor Nigersaurus chose a bad spot to cool off...

Another threat to Nigersaurus was Eocarcharia. This cousin of Giganotosaurus grew to 8 metres in length and had fearsome, bladelike teeth.

Nigersaurus was a special sauropod. It had one of the widest mouths of any dinosaur ever discovered.

Sarcosuchus had two rows of armour plates, called scutes, running along its back.

Just like on a treetrunk, Sarcosuchus's armour plates had growth lines revealing its age. Experts think it may have lived for about 70 years.

**Sarcosuchus**

**Meaning:** 'Flesh crocodile'
**First Fossil Found:** Niger
**Date:** Early Cretaceous

**Group:** Pholidosaurs (related to crocodiles)
**Diet:** Meat and fish
**Size:** 12 metres long

Nigersaurus fed by swinging its long neck back and forth, cropping plants with its unusual mouth, just like a giant lawnmower.

Ténéré Desert

NIGER

The king of crocodiles' powerful jaws contained 132 teeth, which were perfect for grabbing hold of slippery fish and crushing bones.

The bulbous tip of Sarcosuchus's snout may have been an echo chamber to make its mating calls louder.

This killer croc fed on fish, but also ate dinosaurs whenever it got the chance.

Sarcosuchus was more than twice the length of the largest crocodile living today, and about 10 times as heavy, weighing in at 8 tonnes.

The stomach of Sarcosuchus would have contained stones to help it grind down the bones and hides of its victims.

**Spinosaurus**

**Meaning:** 'Spine lizard'
**First Fossil Found:** Egypt
**Date:** Late Cretaceous
**Group:** Spinosaurs
**Diet:** Meat and fish
**Size:** 15 metres long

Spinosaurus had a large sail on its back. It may have used this to control its body temperature, angling it towards or away from the sun to warm up or cool down.

Carcharodontosaurus was another large hunter, whose powerful jaws were lined with teeth up to 20 centimetres long.

Spinosaurus's nostrils were high on its head, so it could dip its snout in the water while still being able to breathe.

## A SPOT OF FISHING WITH THE

# SPINOSAURUS, EGYPT

Today, the country of Egypt is mostly covered in a vast, dry desert. But 95 million years ago, this area was a swampland of marshes, rivers and tropical forests. This watery world was the perfect home for a huge fish-eating predator called Spinosaurus. Even bigger than a T. rex, Spinosaurus was possibly the largest land-based predator ever to walk the planet.

To hunt, Spinosaurus stands in the shallows, lowering its snout beneath the surface. The tip of the snout is covered in sensors, so Spinosaurus can tell when a fish is swimming past. And the fish on the menu today is no light snack – it's an 8-metre-long sawfish: Onchopristis. When its prey draws close, Spinosaurus snaps its jaws shut, seizing the fish between its razor-sharp teeth.

There were enough plants in the forests here to feed herds of huge sauropods, like Paralatitan, who grew up to about 26 metres long.

Unlike many other meat-eaters, who had serrated teeth for slicing through flesh, Spinosaurus had smooth, conical teeth for snaring slippery fish.

The skull of this enormous hunter was nearly 2 metres long, and its jaws were long and narrow, just like a crocodile's.

Spinosaurus might have used its sail for display, flushing it with blood to attract a mate.

It's strange to find two large predators living in the same area, but here, Spinosaurus dominated in the rivers and swamps, while Carcharodontosaurus was the master of the land.

Spinosaurus is one of the only known swimming dinosaurs! It was not particularly nimble on land, but was very comfortable in the water.

Onchopristis was a giant sawfish whose long snout was lined with barbs. It may have used these to rake over the riverbed to find shellfish to eat.

**Feeling feathery with the KULINDADROMEUS (Russia)**

# Russia

**Terrorising the seas with the GINSU SHARK (Kazakhstan)**

**Hiding away with the PSITTICOSAURUS (Russia)**

**Intimidating rivals with the GIGANTORAPTOR (China)**

**Doing battle with the PROTOCERATOPS (Mongolia)**

# Europe

**Sharing the spoils with the ARAMBOURGIANA (Jordan)**

Black Sea

Turkey

Caspian Sea

## Kazakhstan

Uzbekistan

# Mongoli

Kyrgyzstan

**Guarding the nest with the OVIRAPTOR (Mongolia)**

Palestine

Syria

Iraq

Turkmenistan

Tajikistan

# China

Lebanon

Israel

Jordan

**Taking off with the AZHDARCHO (Uzbekistan)**

**Cruising the corals with the ELASMOSAURUS (Israel)**

Kuwait

Iran

Afghanistan

**On the hunt with the RAJASAURUS (India)**

**Breaking records with the MAMENCHISAURUS (China)**

Bahrain

Qatar

Pakistan

Nepal

Bhutan

**India**

**Long-necked living with the TANYSTROPHEUS (Saudi Arabia)**

Bangladesh

Myanmar

## Saudi Arabia

Oman

# India

**Fighting for survival with the ALWALKERIA (India)**

Yemen

# Africa

**Arabian Sea**

Bay of Bengal

**Taking a dip with the SIAMOSAURUS (Thailand)**

Thailand

# Indian Ocean

Sri Lanka

Malaysia

Indone

Maldives

India didn't join up with the rest of Asia until after the age of the dinosaurs. When the collision happened, about 40 million years ago, the Earth's crust buckled to form the Himalayan Mountains.

Seychelles

Chagos Archipelago

# ASIA & THE MIDDLE EAST

**Spectacular fossil discoveries from Asia within the last 20 years have changed the way we think about dinosaurs. China and Mongolia are a fossil-hunter's paradise, revealing some amazing, headline-grabbing feathery finds.**

Making a racket with the CHARONOSAURUS (China)

Taking to the trees with the MICRORAPTOR (China)

Japan

North Korea

South Korea

Grabbing lunch with the FUKUIRAPTOR (Japan)

Bonin Islands

printing with the ORNITHOIDES, (China)

Volcano Islands

Getting a head for heights with the ULTRASAURUS (South Korea)

Taiwan

Blending in with the LUFENGOSAURUS (China)

East China Sea

Since 2006, China has been the world's leading country for dinosaur discoveries. This is because there are many large, dry, rocky areas – perfect for fossils – and recent years have seen a big increase in the number of expert dino-hunters.

South China Sea

Philippines

Laos

Vietnam

Cambodia

Brunei

Sabah

Singapore

Sarawak

Indonesian Borneo

Sulawesi

Celebes

Papua

Java

Sumba

Flores

East Timor

# North Pacific Ocean

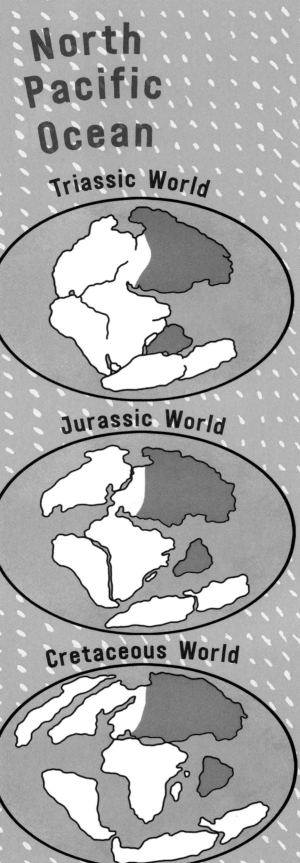

## Triassic World

## Jurassic World

## Cretaceous World

**Sinornithoides**

**Meaning:** 'Chinese bird form'
**First Fossil Found:** China
**Date:** Early Cretaceous
**Group:** Theropods
**Diet:** Meat
**Size:** I metre long

This birdlike dinosaur had a coat of feathers. Scientists think that feathers may have helped a dinosaur stay warm or attract a mate.

The long, flexible tail of Sinornithoides helped it balance and turn while sprinting along.

SPRINTING WITH THE

# SINORNITHOIDES, CHINA

About 113 million years ago, as moonlight floods the plains of Early Cretaceous China, a group of fast-footed Sinornithoides is on the move. These speedy, long-legged creatures are built for running, zooming across the landscape to track down prey.

Although Sinornithoides is small (about the same size as a modern-day turkey), it is large in the brain department. This little dinosaur, a cousin of the Troodon, has a big brain for its size, making it one of the smartest dinosaurs that ever lived. They are agile hunters, too: light and lean. Racing across the plains, the pack-members' large eyes help them see through the gloom. One of the group spots a stirring in the undergrowth and rushes to explore – then the rest close in to feast on a family of small mammals.

Ordos Basin

CHINA

Wuerosaurus was one of the last known stegosaurs to exist — most of its relatives lived earlier, in the Jurassic period.

This armoured dinosaur, called Sauroplites, was an ankylosaur, and was covered in thick, tough plates for protection.

When fossil-hunters found the remains of Sinornithoides in modern-day China, it was curled up in a sleeping pose, with its head tucked under its arm. Aww, sweet!

Sinornithoides had a long sickle-like claw on each foot, which it used for stabbing prey.

Sinornithoides hunted small lizards, insects and mammals, chasing them down on its long legs.

Sinobaatar was a small mammal who would have tried to shelter out of sight of hunters.

# MICRORAPTOR, CHINA

In the shadow of a rumbling volcano 120 million years ago, there's a hunt going on in the forest. A small lizard scampers up a tree, desperate to escape from a hungry dinosaur who is giving chase. But the dinosaur – named Microraptor – will not be so easily defeated. Using her sharp claws, she shimmies up the trunk in pursuit of the lizard. Once up among the leaves, the lizard has a nifty trick to get away...

He sprints along a branch, and then leaps into the air, stretching out his ribs to make a pair of wings, which he uses to glide to a nearby tree. Again, the Microraptor does not give up. She too leaps into the air, her feathered arms and legs splayed out like wings, which allow her to glide after her prey. This little dinosaur's treetop aerobatics make it a formidable hunter, on the ground and in the air. Lookout below!

This bird – named Confuciusornis – had fingers on its wings, just like a pterosaur.

The skies here were full of birds as well as flying reptiles.

The size of a guinea pig, Microraptor is one of the smallest dinosaurs ever discovered.

Caudipteryx was a birdlike dinosaur with long feathers on its arms and tail. It couldn't fly, but perhaps used its feathers to attract a mate, like a modern-day peacock.

This lizard (called Xianglong) had long ribs covered in skin, which stuck out from its sides like a parachute. It could glide up to 50 metres through the air!

**Microraptor**

**Meaning:** 'Small thief'
**First Fossil Found:** China
**Date:** Early Cretaceous
**Group:** Theropods
**Diet:** Meat
**Size:** 0.5 metres long

Some dinosaurs used their feathers to keep warm or to show off, but Microraptor had long, vaned feathers that allowed it to glide distances of up to 18 metres!

Microraptor had no powerful flight muscles, so it couldn't fly for very long, or take off from the ground, but it could glide between the trees.

Large claws on Microraptor's feet would have helped it climb. One toe on each hind foot pointed backwards, as on a bird's foot, so it could perch on branches.

Liaoning Province

CHINA

Microraptor used its long tail to control its glide and help it steer.

Not all reptiles had scaly skin. The discovery of feathered dinosaurs in the 1990s convinced scientists that modern-day birds are directly descended from the dinosaurs.

Liaoxiornis is one of the smallest Cretaceous birds ever discovered. It was about the size of a hummingbird.

Sinosauropteryx was little in size, but big in importance. It was the first feathered dinosaur ever found, and its discovery in 1996 changed the way people thought about dinosaurs.

# HIDING AWAY WITH THE
# PSITTACOSAURUS, RUSSIA

About 120 million years ago, on the outskirts of a lush forest, a family of Psittacosaurus are searching for food. These dinosaurs are related to the Triceratops, but they don't have any fearsome headgear to protect themselves. Instead, they have a different form of defence; one that may not be obvious at first. These dinosaurs are in disguise! Their scaly skin bears markings that camouflage them in the dappled light of the forest.

Like modern-day antelopes, they are dark on top, with light-coloured bellies. This type of pattern means when light falls on them, their shape is harder to see, which helps them hide away. These dinosaurs also have stripes and spots on their legs, which break up their outline and help them blend in with their surroundings, just like a zebra. With these clever means of disguise – as well as their excellent eyesight – the group manage to stay well clear of danger.

Normally, dinosaur fossils don't show what colour a creature would have been. But dino-hunters in China found an amazing Psittacosaurus fossil with the skin preserved. This meant that scientists could make a life-sized model showing how its camouflage worked!

This meat-eating, possum-like mammal, called Gobiconodon, was one of the largest mammals of the time.

Psittacosaurus had a parrot-like beak and horns jutting out from the sides of its face.

Experts think that a young Psittacosaurus would have walked on four legs, while an adult walked upright on two legs.

These small plant-eaters were widespread in Asia. They were fast runners, and lived in groups for protection against hunters.

RUSSIA

Kemerovo

This sauropod, nicknamed Sibirosaurus, grew up to 20 metres long and weighed the same as seven African elephants!

Turtles such as Kirgizemys would have swum in lakes and rivers in Early Cretaceous Russia.

Kyasuchus was a relative of modern-day crocodiles, but it lived on land and chased after small lizards and mammals.

Some species of Psittacosaurus had long quills on their tails, perhaps to attract mates.

**Psittacosaurus**

**Meaning:** 'Parrot lizard'
**First Fossil Found:** Mongolia
**Date:** Early Cretaceous
**Group:** Ceratopsids
**Diet:** Plants
**Size:** 1.5 metres long

**Gigantoraptor**

**Meaning:** 'Giant thief'
**First Fossil Found:** China
**Date:** Late Cretaceous
**Group:** Theropods
**Diet:** Omnivore
**Size:** 8 metres long

This sauropod, called Sonidosaurus, measured about 9 metres long. It was while searching for Sonidosaurus fossils that a Chinese palaeontologist discovered the first Gigantoraptor fossil, by accident.

This small tyrannosaur, Alectrosaurus, prowled the Late Cretaceous deserts. It was smaller than Gigantoraptor but had a deadly bite.

Gigantoraptor had fearsome 20-centimetre-long claws, but it wasn't necessarily a meat-eater. It may have used its toothless beak to bite through leaves or crush eggs and nuts.

Gigantoraptor was closely related to some smaller feathered dinosaurs, but was much, much bigger. The scientist who discovered the fossils in 2007 said it was like finding a mouse the size of a cow!

This huge feathered dino, which looked like an oversized ostrich, was twice as tall as an adult human.

The long legs of Gigantoraptor would have helped it sprint across the desert.

Inner
Mongolia

CHINA

The largest dino eggs ever found, measuring over 45 centimetres long, are thought to have belonged to Gigantoraptor.

Bactrosaurus was a type of hadrosaur that would have munched plants while listening out for predators.

**INTIMIDATING RIVALS WITH THE**

# GIGANTORAPTOR, CHINA

About 80 million years ago, among the sand dunes of what is now the Gobi Desert in Inner Mongolia, a couple of dinosaurs are squaring up for a fight. Meet Gigantoraptor, one of the largest feathered creatures that ever lived. This enormous dinosaur has feathered arms – but it can't fly. Instead, Gigantoraptor uses its feathers for display.

This pair of males are trying to impress a female. They strut and preen – each attempting to show off his strength. They puff up their feathers to look threatening, and then bow down low in a feathery display. The two males flap and peck at each other until eventually the smaller one tires and retreats, leaving the larger male to his prize.

KAZAKHSTAN

Mangyshlak
Peninsula

Xiphactinus could open its huge jaws wide enough to swallow a 2-metre-long fish in one gulp.

The Ginsu shark roamed oceans across the globe: it was first discovered in North America.

Measuring up to 7 metres long, the Ginsu shark was one of the largest sharks living in the Late Cretaceous seas.

This terrifying shark killed deadly mosasaurs by violently twisting their heads!

Fossil-hunters have discovered the remains of a Ginsu shark with a partly digested Xiphactinus fish in its stomach. Yum!

# GINSU SHARK, KAZAKHSTAN

During the Cretaceous period about 85 million years ago, a warm, shallow sea covered much of what is now Asia. Powering through this ancient ocean was a terrifying creature: Cretoxyrhina. This shark, nicknamed the Ginsu shark after a type of knife that slices and dices, was as large as the modern-day great white shark. With its streamlined body, powerful tail and mouth full of razor-sharp teeth, the Ginsu shark was a killing machine that was perfectly equipped for hunting in these prehistoric waters.

This hunter of hunters preyed not only on smaller sea creatures, but also on deadly mosasaurs and other sharks.

This Ginsu shark has a monstrous meal on the menu. It is on the hunt for an enormous fish named Xiphactinus, which is a terrifying creature! It is five metres long and has massive jaws lined with fang-like teeth. It is fast, too – with a top speed of around 60 kilometres per hour. But with the chance to bag a huge meal, the Ginsu shark can be just as speedy, slicing through the Cretaceous waters after its prey.

The knife-like teeth of the Ginsu shark measured up to 7 centimetres long, and could crunch through bone.

Sharks have swum in the world's oceans for nearly 450 million years. They were around 200 million years before the dinosaurs!

Another creature on the Ginsu shark's menu was Platecarpus. This mosasaur was about 4 metres long and weaved through the water like a snake.

Platypterygius was a 7-metre-long ichthyosaur with a powerful tail. The long snouts of the ichthyosaurs made them look like modern-day dolphins.

**Ginsu Shark**

| | |
|---|---|
| **Meaning:** 'Cretaceous sharp nose' | **Group:** Sharks |
| **First Fossil Found:** USA | **Diet:** Meat and fish |
| **Date:** Late Cretaceous | **Size:** 7 metres long |

**Oviraptor**

**Meaning:** 'Egg thief'
**First Fossil Found:** Mongolia
**Date:** Late Cretaceous

**Group:** Theropods
**Diet:** Omnivore
**Size:** 2 metres long

Pinacosaurus was a type of dinosaur called an ankylosaur. It had thick armour to protect itself, as well as a big club on the end of its tail.

Velociraptor was a small, nimble meat-eater with sharp claws that could slash through thick skin.

Oviraptor parents hunted for food for their chicks. They may have fed the chicks partly digested food, just as birds do today.

This speedy, feathery little hunter may have prowled in packs, searching for prey.

Scientists think that dinosaur babies took between three and six months to hatch from their eggs.

GUARDING THE NEST WITH THE

# OVIRAPTOR, MONGOLIA

Seventy-two million years ago, as the wind whips across the desert dunes of what is now Mongolia, this Oviraptor father is protecting his nest, on the lookout for hunters. This dinosaur was named because of a misunderstanding. When its fossils were first found, it was lying next to a nest of eggs thought to belong to a Protoceratops, so it was named 'egg thief'. But now, experts think that it wasn't stealing eggs after all, but looking after its own nest! Some dinosaurs buried their eggs, then left them to hatch alone, but others – like Oviraptor – looked after the eggs and the chicks for several months, until they were old enough to fend for themselves. Oviraptor was similar in size to an ostrich and – just like an ostrich today – the males as well as the females may have guarded the nest. This Oviraptor has spotted some Velociraptors on the prowl. He flattens himself against the sand, hoping they won't spot him. But, if they come too close, he will scare them off, hissing, flapping and brandishing his sharp talons.

In 1971, fossil-hunters in the Gobi Desert made an amazing find: the remains of a Velociraptor and a Protoceratops locked in a fight! These dinosaurs were smothered by a collapsing sand dune.

Protoceratops had a large head frill and a sharp beak, which it used to defend itself.

Oviraptor had a strong beak with sharp spikes on the roof of its mouth. It could have used these to crack open other dinosaurs' eggs to eat.

Oviraptors may have held their feathered tails upright, shaking them around to scare off attackers or impress mates.

MONGOLIA

Nemegt Basin

Fossil-hunters have found the remains of Oviraptors guarding their nests, who were buried alive by desert sandstorms!

Charonosaurus was a type of plant-eating dinosaur called a hadrosaur. Hadrosaurs were also known as the duck-billed dinosaurs, because of their bony beaks.

Different types of hadrosaur sported different-shaped head crests, which would have made different sounds. A hadrosaur would have recognised the call of its own species.

A close cousin of the mighty T. rex, Tarbosaurus was a large hunter who grew to about 12 metres long, with a mouthful of razor-sharp teeth. Grrrrrr!

Youngsters had smaller crests. They made higher-pitched sounds than the adults, whose voices deepened over time.

## MAKING A RACKET WITH THE
# CHARONOSAURUS, CHINA

In the sweltering midday heat 66 million years ago, in what is now northeast China, a herd of Charonosaurus are cooling off at a watering hole. Some are having a drink and some are taking a dip, while others munch the waterside plants. One of the good things about living in a herd is that there are more eyes to spot danger. And when danger draws close, this dinosaur has an unusual way of sounding the alarm: it belts out a loud trumpeting noise, like an elephant, from the hollow crest on top of its head!

On the edge of the group, one of the Charonosaurus notices an approaching predator: the fierce hunter Tarbosaurus. The lookout alerts the others, blowing through his trombone-like crest to bellow out a warning call. At once, the herd springs into action. The bathers emerge, dripping, from the water and join the others as they make a speedy exit, honking and blowing in panic. When Tarbosaurus arrives at the watering hole, his dinner will have vanished. Better luck next time!

Many other hadrosaurs lived in this area at the end of the Cretaceous period, including Amurosaurus.

Olorotitan was a large hadrosaur with a fan-shaped head crest.

**Charonosaurus**

**Meaning:** 'Charon's lizard'
**First Fossil Found:** China
**Date:** Late Cretaceous

**Group:** Hadrosaurs
**Diet:** Plants
**Size:** 10 metres long

Scientists once thought a hadrosaur's head crest was a type of snorkel! But without an air hole in the top, this snorkel wouldn't have been much good...

Charonosaurus may have used its large head crest to make mating calls, as well as warning calls.

Charonosaurus is one of the largest hadrosaurs discovered in Asia.

Heilongjiang Province

CHINA

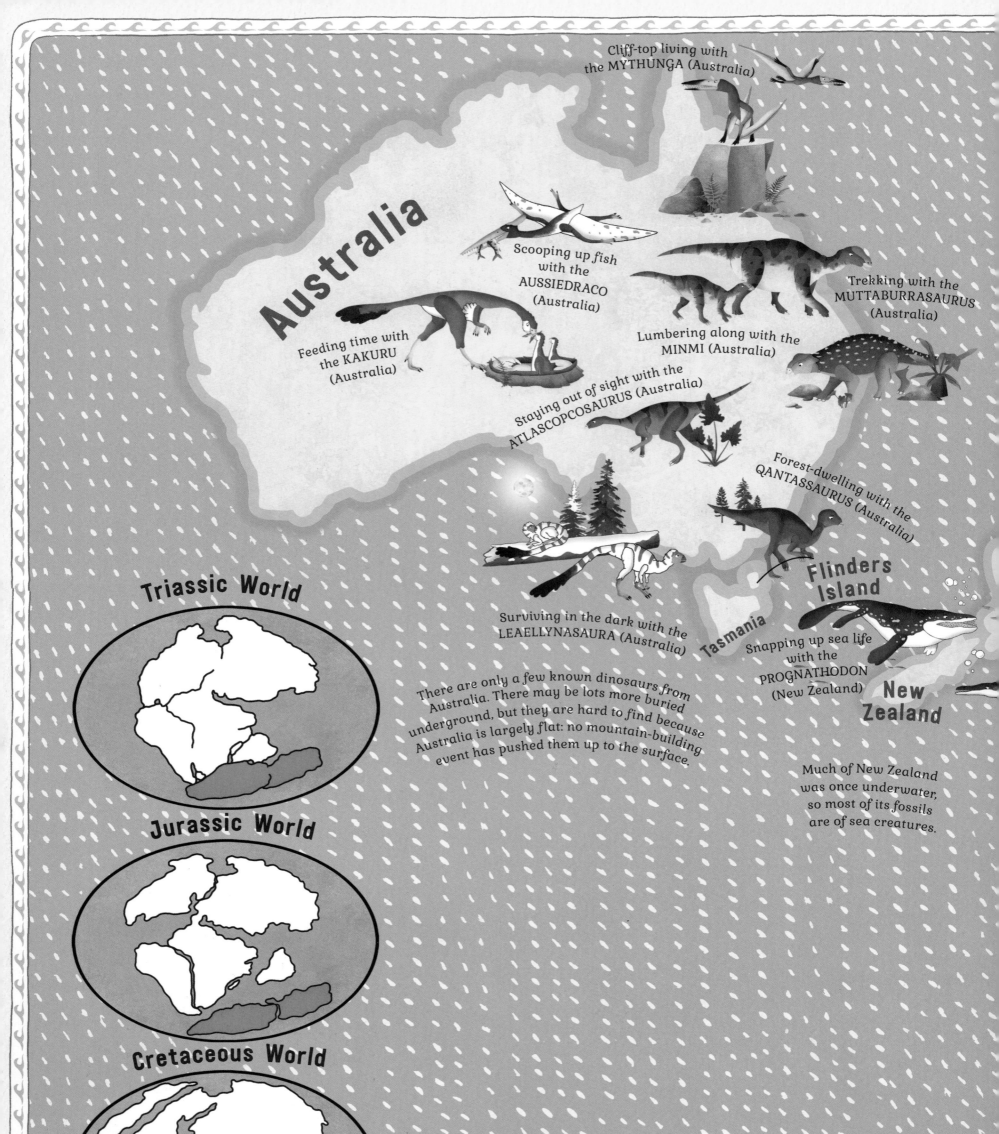

Cliff-top living with
the MYTHUNGA (Australia)

# Australia

Scooping up fish
with the
AUSSIEDRACO
(Australia)

Trekking with the
MUTTABURRASAURUS
(Australia)

Feeding time with
the KAKURU
(Australia)

Lumbering along with the
MINMI (Australia)

Staying out of sight with the
ATLASCOPCOSAURUS (Australia)

Forest-dwelling with the
QANTASSAURUS (Australia)

Flinders
Island

Surviving in the dark with the
LEAELLYNASAURA (Australia)

Tasmania

Snapping up sea life
with the
PROGNATHODON
(New Zealand)

New
Zealand

There are only a few known dinosaurs from
Australia. There may be lots more buried
underground, but they are hard to find because
Australia is largely flat: no mountain-building
event has pushed them up to the surface.

Much of New Zealand
was once underwater,
so most of its fossils
are of sea creatures.

## Triassic World

## Jurassic World

## Cretaceous World

# AUSTRALASIA & ANTARCTICA

**During the period when dinosaurs roamed the Earth, Australia and New Zealand were joined to Antarctica. Temperatures in the region weren't nearly as cold as they are today, but the creatures that lived here still had to be versatile and tough enough to survive the long, dark and chilly South Polar winters.**

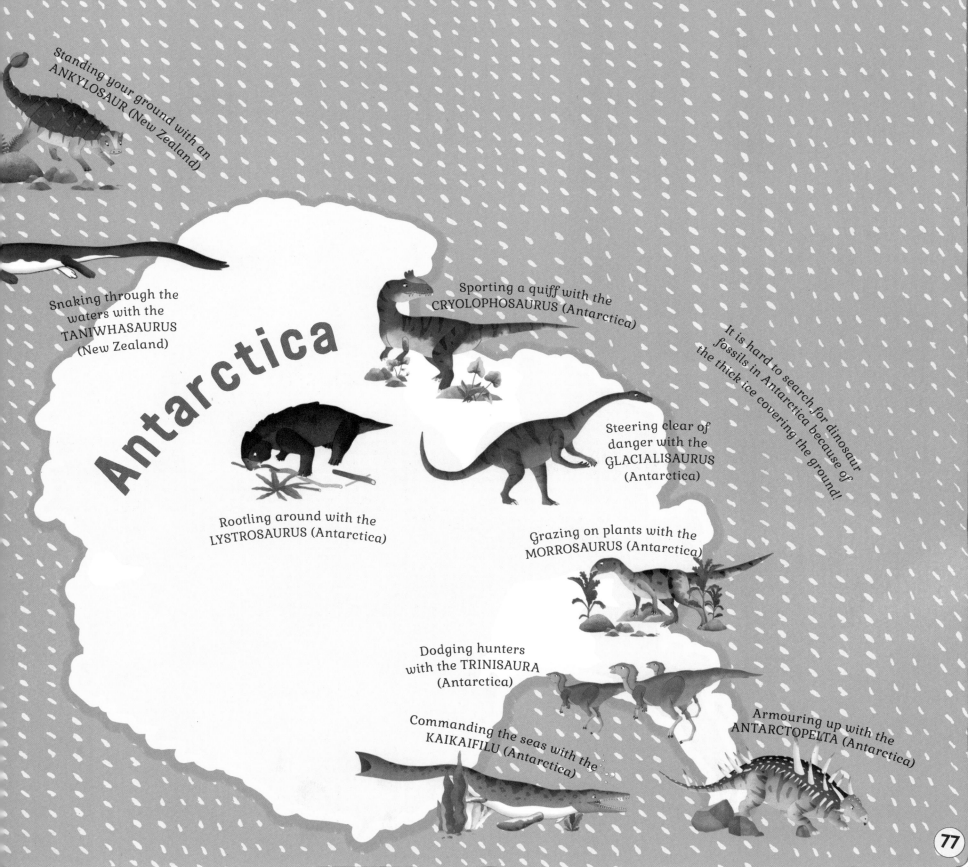

Standing your ground with an ANKYLOSAUR (New Zealand)

Snaking through the waters with the TANIWHASAURUS (New Zealand)

Sporting a quiff with the CRYOLOPHOSAURUS (Antarctica)

It is hard to search for dinosaur fossils in Antarctica because of the thick ice covering the ground!

Antarctica

Steering clear of danger with the GLACIALISAURUS (Antarctica)

Rootling around with the LYSTROSAURUS (Antarctica)

Grazing on plants with the MORROSAURUS (Antarctica)

Dodging hunters with the TRINISAURA (Antarctica)

Commanding the seas with the KAIKAIFILU (Antarctica)

Armouring up with the ANTARCTOPELTA (Antarctica)

AUSTRALIA

Dinosaur Cove

Many of the dinosaurs that lived in the polar forest during the winter were small: they couldn't migrate north like larger dinosaurs, because it used up too much energy.

Atlascopcosaurus was another small plant-eater who lived in these polar forests. It had long legs, so was probably a fast runner.

This huge amphibian, Koolasuchus, survived in southern lakes and rivers for millions of years.

These Leaellynasaura may have built up their body fat during the summer to keep them warm in winter, just as polar animals do today.

## SURVIVING IN THE DARK WITH THE
# LEAELLYNASAURA, AUSTRALIA

About 115 million years ago, Australia was joined to Antarctica and was much closer to the South Pole than it is today. Earth was warmer than it is now so, instead of Antarctic ice caps, the land was covered in lush forests. But during the winter, the continent was in total darkness for months on end, with temperatures falling below freezing. Luckily, Leaellynasaura were small but tough.

They were built to survive in this extreme climate. During the cold, dark winter, they sheltered within the forest, their large eyes helping them see through the gloom. These clever, sociable little creatures had big brains for their size and lived in small groups. They were at risk from other dinosaurs and from swooping pterosaurs, so one of the clan had to be on the lookout at all times.

If a sentry spotted danger, he would make a warning call to alert the rest of the clan.

**Leaellynasaura**

**Meaning:** 'Leaellyn's lizard'
**First Fossil Found:** Australia
**Date:** Early Cretaceous

**Group:** Ornithopods
**Diet:** Plants
**Size:** 1 metre long

Timimus was an agile meat-eater who may have hunted young Leaellynasaura.

The Leaellynasaura's tail was three times the length of the rest of its body! It may have been covered in feathers and used for display.

As well as eating plants, the Leaellynasaura may also have snacked on insects, such as woodlice, to keep it going during the winter.

The Leaellynasaura was named after Leaellyn, the daughter of the husband-and-wife palaeontologists who discovered it.

Leaellynasaura may have had a coat of feathers to keep it warm. Some experts think that it wrapped its long tail around itself, like a scarf, when sleeping!

AUSTRALIA Queensland

Mythunga was a fish-hunting pterosaur who would have cruised the coastlines of Cretaceous Australia.

Muttaburrasaurus had a large bulge on its snout, which it probably used to make honking sounds to communicate with members of its herd.

A male Muttaburrasaurus may have inflated his nose bulge to impress the females in mating season.

These dinosaurs walked on all fours, but would have stood on their hind legs to reach juicy leaves.

Muttaburrasaurus was closely related to the Iguanodon. Both come from the ornithopod group of dinosaurs (which means 'bird-footed').

The fossils of Muttaburrasaurus were discovered by a cattle-farmer on his ranch near the town of Muttaburra in the 1960s.

### Muttaburrasaurus

**Meaning:** 'Muttaburra lizard'
**First Fossil Found:** Australia
**Date:** Early Cretaceous
**Group:** Ornithopods
**Diet:** Plants
**Size:** 7 metres long

Australovenator was a speedy, 5-metre-long meat-eater with large slashing claws and sharp teeth. Scary!

Muttaburrasaurus was a muscular, solid dinosaur. A large adult may have weighed 3 tonnes — heavier than a modern-day rhino!

Minmi was a tanklike dinosaur called an ankylosaur. Too slow to escape from predators, it depended on its tough armour for defence.

If a Muttaburrasaurus wanted to escape from a predator, it may have been able to sprint away on its hind legs.

## TREKKING WITH THE
# MUTTABURRASAURUS, AUSTRALIA

In what is now eastern Australia, 100 million years ago, the polar forest has been in total darkness for many months of winter. But now, spring is creeping across the landscape: plants are budding and temperatures are rising. Soon, the long, dark winter will be replaced by months of 24-hour sunlight.

As spring comes to the forest, a herd of Muttaburrasaurus is on the move. They are beginning an 800-kilometre trek to the south, following the sun to find food and safe sites to lay their eggs. Along the way, they travel through thick forest, calling out to each other to stay in touch. These plant-eaters are feeding machines, able to stand on their hind legs and shear leaves from tall plants and bushy trees with their powerful teeth. When they have stripped an entire area bare, they will move on, heading further south to find more food. And when, at last, winter returns, they will begin their long journey back north again.

**Antarctopelta**

**Meaning:** 'Antarctic shield'
**First Fossil Found:** Antarctica
**Date:** Late Cretaceous

**Group:** Ankylosaurs
**Diet:** Plants
**Size:** 4 metres long

The harsh conditions of Antarctica make tough work for fossil-hunters: glacial temperatures, biting winds and frozen ground meant that the remains of Antarctopelta took 10 years to excavate!

Many types of ankylosaur had a powerful club on the end of their tails, which could shatter a predator's knee. However, Antarctopelta probably didn't have a tail club.

Some species of ankylosaur were so well protected that they even had armoured eyelids!

This small plant-eater, called Trinisaura, would have scampered around on its hind legs, grazing on foliage and keeping an eye out for predators.

ARMOURING UP WITH THE

# ANTARCTOPELTA, ANTARCTICA

Seventy million years ago, Antarctica was much milder than it is today and was covered in green woodland, where dinosaurs roamed. But because most of this now-frozen continent is cloaked in thick ice and snow, fossil-hunting is a tricky job. In 1986 on a remote island, scientists made an amazing discovery: the first Antarctic dinosaur! This tanklike creature, an ankylosaur called Antarctopelta, was protected from head to tail by bony plates of tough armour.

A pack of small meat-eaters have surrounded this lone Antarctopelta. It may be only 4 metres long, but it is still a force to be reckoned with. Its bony plates help shield it from sharp, biting teeth, while its stocky, muscular form and short legs keep it low to the ground – protecting its belly. And as if that isn't enough, it has sharp spikes jutting out from the sides of its body, threatening to impale would-be attackers. These hunters had better try their luck elsewhere...

This part of Antarctica was connected to South America in the Cretaceous period.

James Ross Island

ANTARCTICA

This speedy little meat-eater was a type of dromaeosaur. It was about 2 metres tall, with sharp, sickle-shaped talons on its back feet.

The dinosaur fossils found on James Ross Island come from rocks that used to be underwater. These dinosaurs probably got washed out to sea after they died.

Mighty reptiles cruised the seas of prehistoric Antarctica. This 10-metre-long mosasaur, named Kaikaifilu, was one of the top predators in these waters.

Long-necked plesiosaurs also swam in the Antarctic waters. This baby plesiosaur would have made an easy snack for Kaikaifilu.

Kaikaifilu powered through the water using its paddle-like limbs and long tail.

The meteorite hit Earth at a time when there were lots of volcanic eruptions. Many scientists believe that these two things combined led to the mass extinction.

The meteorite made a crater more than 185 kilometres across!

Scientists think that the 10-kilometre-wide meteorite smashed into what is now eastern Mexico at a speed of 100,000 kilometres per hour.

The pterosaurs, large marine reptiles and big dinosaurs died out, but some smaller creatures, such as mammals and insects, managed to survive.

Some small, feathered dinosaurs also lived on, evolving into the birds we see around us today.

Dinosaurs that lived within 1,000 kilometres of the impact would have been killed immediately by the burning fireball. However, it may have taken hundreds or even thousands of years for the effects of the impact to devastate the rest of the world.

# WHAT HAPPENED TO THE DINOSAURS?

Dinosaurs lived on Earth for 160 million years, which is a long time. Humans, on the other hand, have only been around for 2 million years – a fraction of that time! About 65 million years ago, the dinosaurs died out. What happened? Why did the dinosaurs disappear? Experts think that a massive meteorite collided with our planet, leading to a mass extinction that wiped out most of life on Earth.

The force of the impact vaporised the meteorite, sending an enormous plume of hot gas into the air, and triggered earthquakes and tsunamis around the world. Molten debris from the explosion started huge fires, and a vast dust cloud blocked out the sun. With no sunlight, the world's plants died, so the plant-eating dinosaurs starved to death, followed by the meat-eaters who preyed on them.

# INDEX

Quarto is the authority on a wide range of topics.
Quarto educates, entertains and enriches the lives of
our readers—enthusiasts and lovers of hands-on living.
www.quartoknows.com

First published in Great Britain in 2017 by Wide Eyed Editions,
an imprint of The Quarto Group, The Old Brewery, Blundell Street, London N7 9BH
QuartoKnows.com
Visit our blogs at QuartoKnows.com

A catalogue record for this book is available from the British Library.

ISBN 978-1-78603-034-4

Illustrated with coloured inks

Set in Festivo, Gabriela and Gill Sans Shadow

Consultant: Dr Jonathan Tennant PhD
Designed by Karissa Santos
Edited by Rebecca Fry and Eryl Nash
Published by Rachel Williams

Printed in China

1 3 5 7 9 8 6 4 2

MIX
Paper from
responsible sources
FSC® C104723

FSC
www.fsc.org

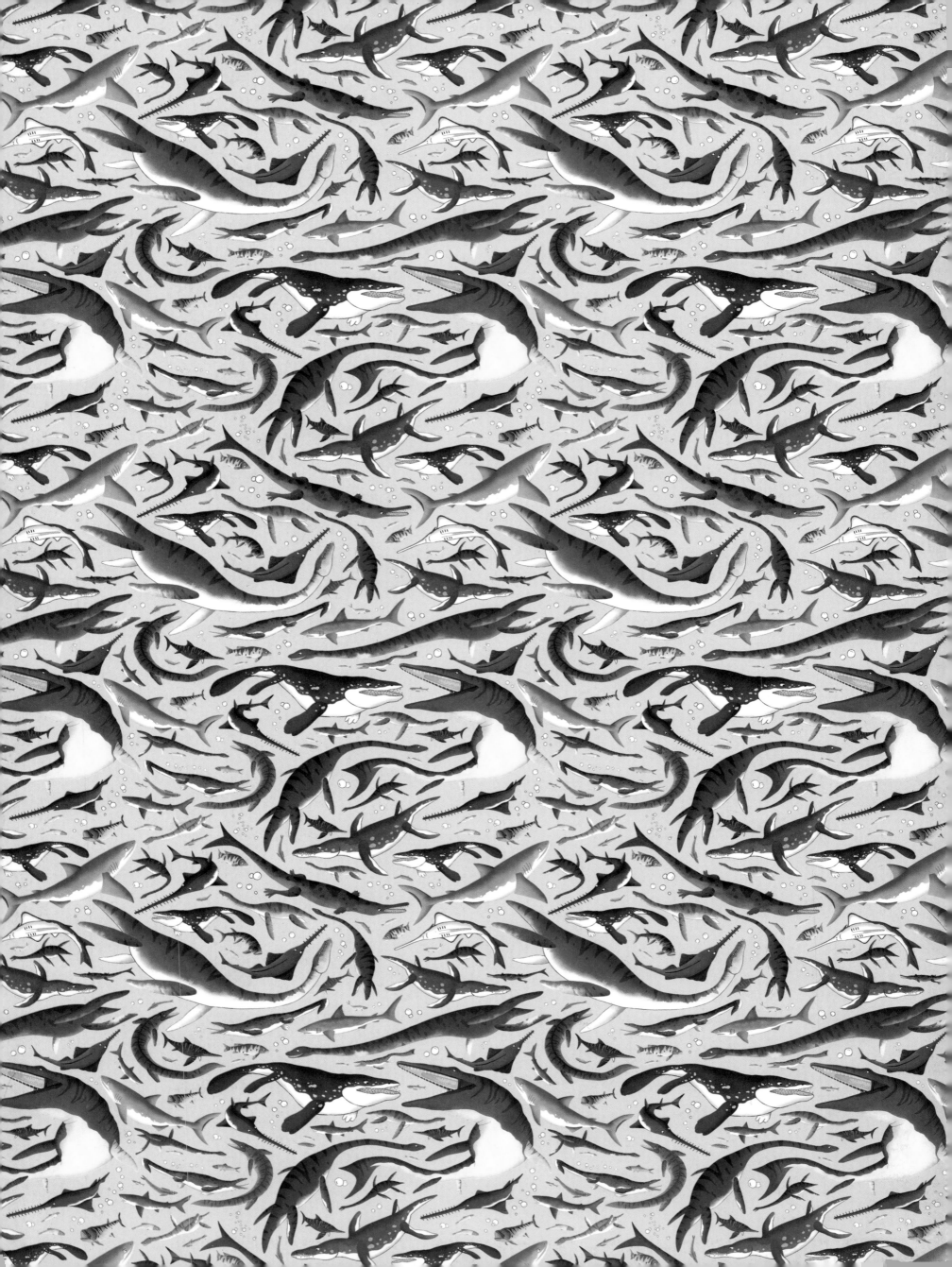